THE TRIALS OF THE LANCASHIRE WITCHES

A Study of Seventeenth-Century Witchcraft

By EDGAR PEEL and PAT SOUTHERN

Drawings by Pat Southern

TAPLINGER PUBLISHING COMPANY
NEW YORK

First published in the United States in 1970 by

TAPLINGER PUBLISHING CO., INC

New York, New York

Copyright © EDGAR PEEL AND PAT SOUTHERN 1969

ISBN 0–8008–7890–6

Library of Congress Catalog Card Number 72–84973

SECOND PRINTING

Printed in Great Britain

Contents

Illustrations

Preface

IN 1954 I was appointed, for the summer months, warden of Whitehough Camp School. This school is used by the boys and girls of Nelson and Colne, the last towns on a long finger of East Lancashire industry which here probes into the Pennines. Its purpose is to give the children a chance to clear their lungs of soot and breathe the fresh air of the countryside, and to this end it is delightfully situated in the valley of the Pendle Water within a mile or two of Pendle Hill.

It was the wettest summer since records began but the new problems and the everchanging faces, as school succeeded school for their allotted fortnights, were a refreshing break from the security of the classroom; and during this season at Whitehough I came under the spell of this lovely part of Lancashire and its most notorious inhabitants—the Lancashire Witches.

In October, after the last batch of boys and girls had hung their sodden tents on the rafters and gone home, a week-end course for teachers was organised under the all-embracing title 'Field Studies' and I was called upon to give the last of three evening lectures. My two colleagues set a high standard. John Jackson, who had been in charge at Whitehough for the season before mine, and is at present warden of the CCPR's Snowdonia Centre at Plas Y Brenin, took us on a spectacular photographic tour of the Garwhal Himalayas, from which he had just returned. Next evening, Alan Brindle, now Keeper of Entomology at Manchester Museum, set up a micro-projector and comfortably filled in his allotted time with the unwitting

9

help of several lively creatures from pond and stream who either fought, mated, or ate each other, on a large white screen before us.

My own contribution, a lecture on the Lancashire Witches, unadorned by slides or live specimens, was nevertheless well received. I was asked to repeat it a week or two later for Nelson Naturalists and before long I had joined that band of unpaid speakers who supply the winter evening needs of Women's Institutes, Round Tables, Ladies' Circles and the like. Nearly always, in the questions and discussions which usually followed, some new fact was forthcoming, and this lecturing kept alive my interest and added to my knowledge of witchcraft and witches.

Four years ago I was introduced to Pat Southern from Barrowford, then an art student at Leeds. An uncle had given her an old copy of Ainsworth's *Lancashire Witches* and this had kindled a curiosity and interest which culminated in a thesis written on witchcraft in general but with particular reference to our local brood. When eventually our paths crossed we discovered that our researches had followed similar lines and led us to the same conclusions. We decided to continue our investigations in partnership and co-operate in the writing of a book which she would illustrate, setting out to present a serious, but not solemn, account of the Lancashire Witch Trials of 1612.

Such an account would have little meaning without an explanation of what witchcraft meant to our forefathers, and some mention of the sources from which their ideas had come, so we include as much about the subject in general as is necessary to make the trials understandable.

The book will, we hope, correct some of the misconceptions current about witchcraft in general and the Lancashire Witches in particular. Many of these notions, based as they are on fiction, legend and occasional articles in the papers, are so vague and inaccurate as to make a serious student wince. Nowhere, we regretfully found, are they more firmly held than among those who live within the shadow of Pendle Hill.

E.P.

CHAPTER I

The Witches and their Chronicler

THE Lancashire Witches is the name given to the men and women arrested in or near Pendle Forest, taken to trial at Lancaster and, with the exception of one who died, either acquitted, imprisoned, or hanged there in August 1612.

Pendle Forest was not a wood. The word 'forest' simply implied an area originally set aside for hunting. It is because most of the people arrested lived there and nearly all their supposed mischief was performed within its bounds that they are equally well known as the Pendle Witches.

They were apprehended and tried under an English law of 1604 for practising the devilish art of witchcraft and by the force of the same killing or laming many of their neighbours or harming their cattle. This law made hanging mandatory for many of the offences of which the juries found them guilty and to which some of them had indeed confessed.

The Lancaster trial was typical of many which occupied the courts about this time, and the crimes with which the accused were charged, the conduct of the trial, and the sentences of death which followed them were very similar to those of the numerous witch trials of the period. Yet these are undoubtedly the most famous witches in English history.

There are several reasons for this, the primary one being that the judges at the Assizes instructed their clerk, Thomas Potts, to make a record of the trials and this was published as a book in 1613 under the title:

THE WONDERFVLL DISCOVERIE OF WITCHES IN THE COVNTIE OF LANCASTER.

With the Arraignement and Triall of Nineteene notorious WITCHES, at the Assizes and generall Gaole deliuerie, holden at the Castle of LANCASTER, vpon Munday, the seuenteenth of August last, 1612.

Potts' reporting of the proceedings was thorough. It had been a large trial and although the numbers involved did not, as he claimed, exceed those of any previous witch trial, it had attracted to Lancaster enormous crowds, drawn no doubt by the ghoulish prospect of seeing so many witches choking on the gallows. Yet eventually, once its immediate impact had subsided, the trial was forgotten; and the book which had recorded it, the *Discovery of Witches*, lay overlooked. As evidence of this, in 1801,

The 'witch's grave' at Newchurch in Pendle. This is not, as local legend would have it, the resting-place of Alice Nutter

when Whitaker's voluminous *History of Whalley* was published, the witches of 1612 were not even mentioned, despite the fact that the author covered the whole of Pendle Forest.

Then about 1810, Potts' book was given a new life and re-published in a collection of 'Scarce and Valuable Tracts'. This series was edited and arranged by Sir Walter Scott who described the *Discovery* as a curious and rare book.

However, the real revival of the Lancashire Witches' fame undoubtedly came halfway through the nineteenth century, and owed its beginnings to the friendship between James Crossley the scholarly head of a Manchester Historical Society, and Harrison Ainsworth, a writer of historical novels. Crossley was president of the Chetham Society. This was founded at his home in 1843, and was subsequently responsible for the printing of many historical documents, including in 1845 the *Discovery of Witches*. Now Crossley was a solicitor, whose partner's son, the same Harrison Ainsworth, had deserted the law to find eventual fame as an author. Ainsworth was already well established when his novel *The Lancashire Witches* was published in 1848, but his debt to his friend is acknowledged in this dedication, which introduces early editions of the book:

> To James Crossley, Esq. of Manchester, president of the Chetham Society, and learned editor of 'The Discovery of Witches in the County of Lancaster', the groundwork of the following pages, this romance, undertaken at his suggestion, is inscribed by his old and sincerely attached friend, the author.

During its writing Ainsworth spent some time in the Pendle district. He stayed with a relative who had a house at Whalley and was also a guest at Newchurch vicarage. His novel re-kindled public interest and we must acknowledge our debt to him for this. It is only unfortunate that until quite recently it was the sole foundation for many people's entire knowledge of the Lancashire Witches. Few heeded, if they read it, the key word in his dedication—'romance'.

As a consequence of the revived interest, in Baines' *History of*

Lancashire, published in 1868, we find a good summary of Potts, and in subsequent editions of Whitaker's *Whalley*, to make up for earlier omissions, editors included the story as a lengthy footnote.

The word 'witch' has been used to describe so many different things. Witchcraft was mentioned in the Bible. Saul's consultations with the witch of Endor are recorded in the first book of Samuel. In Exodus is the famous edict 'Thou shalt not suffer a witch to live'. Not many generations ago witches were frequently burnt as evildoers. Witchcraft survives and witch doctors still practise in Africa, and from the publicity they manage to attract there must be very few people who have not read of the existence of witches in Britain today. Behind all these is the pervasive image of the old crone with her broomstick and cat, her toad and cauldron.

Yet the women of the Old Testament, the witches who drew crowds to their executions, the African with his bones and charms against the evil eye, the fairytale witch, and those whose naked frolics that regularly scandalise the chaste reporters of *The People* and *News of the World*, have little, if any, connection with each other. It is those in the second category, the poor wretches, men, women and children, who were persecuted and cruelly and publicly put to death in Europe, not so many hundred years ago, with whom the Lancashire Witches must be classed.

As the term came to be understood in the sixteenth and seventeenth centuries, witches were supposed to have made a contract with the Devil, and usually to have committed the ultimate debauchery of having sexual relations with him, in one of his many guises. Details of the ceremonies at which Satan sealed the covenant were soon invented, and in a few continental trials, a written document, impressively signed in blood by the Devil himself, was produced as evidence. Once this unlikely pact, the absolute essence of witch belief, had been defined, and naturally declared a heresy by the Church, nothing was considered too impossible, ridiculous or obscene to be attributed to witches.

A witch can be either a man or a woman, and the terms wizard and warlock should not be used to describe men. Although we conclude that those who concern us were innocent of any serious crime, and had little connection with the craft to which they were supposed to belong, we shall continue, for the sake of simplicity, to call them witches, and usually, unless it is obviously a man who is under discussion, continue to use the pronoun 'she'.

More than a hundred years after Ainsworth's *Lancashire Witches*, by which time its Victorian style was undoubtedly repelling many would-be readers, interest was again revived by Robert Neill's *Mist over Pendle*. Although a novel again, it gives a much more realistic picture of the events of the times, and for most of us today it is an infinitely more readable book. All who try to tell this story, whether as a novel or as plain history, must draw on Potts' chronicle of the trials, and the thanks of all of us were well expressed by Robert Neill, who dedicated *Mist over Pendle*:

To the dusty memory of MASTER THOMAS POTTS, Sometime Clerk to the Judges in The Circuit of the North Parts Who in November, 1612, at his Lodging in Chancery Lane, wrote of the Late WONDERFUL DISCOVERIE OF WITCHES in the Countie of Lancaster.

CHAPTER II

Witchcraft in Pendle Forest

ABOUT the year 1595, at Christmas time, Christopher Nutter was travelling home from Burnley with his two sons, Robert and John. They lived with their womenfolk at Greenhead, a fine house only about two miles from the town but within the bounds of Pendle Forest. On their land, in a dwelling much humbler than their own, lived an old woman of seventy, Anne Whittle, nicknamed Chattox, a widow, sharing a home with her daughter, also called Anne, her daughter's husband Thomas Redfearn and one or two others of the family. The actual words which passed between the three men, on this winter journey so many years ago, have come down to us through the pages of Potts' book.

John Nutter was unwell and he was assuring his father that he was bewitched by Chattox and her daughter.

'I pray you,' he said, 'cause them to be laid in Lancaster Castle.' But his father refused.

'Thou art a foolish lad, it is not so, it is thy miscarriage,' he told him. Still the younger man insisted that he was bewitched.

'If ever I come again,' he said, 'I will have them laid where they shall be glad to bite lice in two with their teeth.'

John Nutter was a retainer of Sir Richard Shuttleworth of nearby Gawthorpe, Chief Justice of Chester for ten years from 1589. He was about to leave with his master for Chester and a circuit in North Wales and before his departure from Green head he threatened Redfearn that when he returned he would

16

Greenhead, where Robert Nutter, his sons and their womenfolk lived in 1595

get his father to put him out of his house, failing which he would pull it down himself. Redfearn replied saying, 'When you come back again you will be in better mind.'

But John Nutter never came back. He died in Cheshire on his way home. Soon after his father fell sick, languished for three months, from Maudlintide to Michaelmas, then died. During his illness Christopher Nutter, who had refused his son's request to deal with Chattox and her daughter, several times assured those around his bed that he was bewitched, but named nobody as the person bewitching him. These deaths by witchcraft, within a short time of each other, of the Nutters, father and son, were the earliest of the sixteen or so which came to light when serious inquiries were initiated eighteen or nineteen years later.

A few miles from Greenhead, and only just within the limit of Pendle Forest, lived another old woman, Elizabeth Southerns, alias Old Demdike, of similar age and condition to Chattox. Her dwelling was called Malkin Tower and with her there lived her daughter Elizabeth, Elizabeth's husband John Device,* and their children. Some few years after the deaths of the Nutters, Malkin Tower was broken into and some clothing and half a peck of cut oatmeal, to the total value of twenty shillings or thereabouts, was stolen. On the Sunday after the theft Alizon Device, Elizabeth's daughter, then a young girl, saw a cap, part of the stolen goods, being worn by one of Chattox's daughters. Anne Redfearn had a sister Bessie: it could have been either of them.

Afraid that his family would suffer further at the hands of Chattox, John Device covenanted with her, that if she would hurt none of them she should have a yearly gift of meal (an aghendole, an obsolete measure, probably about eight pounds). In the first year in which this bribe was not paid John Device died, upon his deathbed saying that Chattox had bewitched him to death for his omission. One wonders why the Demdikes were in fear of the Chattoxes and had to submit to their persecution as they themselves were reputedly witches.

On John Device's death, his widow Elizabeth was left with three children, Alizon, James, and the youngest, Jennet. The boy was later described as a labourer but they seem to have lived principally by begging, for which pursuit magistrates had authority in those days to grant licences. As old Demdike became blind it fell to Alizon to lead her grandmother when she went abroad. About 1610 Elizabeth Device had done some work for Richard Baldwin who owned a mill at Wheathead. Having, she considered, been insufficiently rewarded for this, she bade her mother go to see Baldwin and ask him for more.

---

* Spelt this way by Potts, probably pronounced 'Davies' and in fact written 'Davies' in 1633 when the family made another brief appearance in Pendle Forest history.

As Old Demdike, led by Alizon, approached Baldwin's house, he met them, and whether in anger or fear, ordered 'Get out of my ground, whores and witches. I will burn the one of you and hang the other.'

'I care not for thee,' retorted Demdike, 'hang thyself.' Very soon after this unpleasant encounter the miller's little daughter became ill, slowly declined and some twelve months later died.

Still, despite what Potts describes as 'a general murmuring of the populace', no action was taken by the people of Pendle Forest against the witches in their midst. Their begging was tolerated and whilst others over the years had cause to charge them with witchcraft there were those who were willing to employ them in various undemanding jobs, and even seek their help and use the powers they were thought to possess in, for instance, curing sick cattle.

The incident which sparked off the whole process of official enquiry and eventual action took place outside Pendle Forest, in Colne. On 18 March 1612 Alizon Device, apparently alone, passed through there on her way to Trawden Forest to beg. This, like Pendle Forest, was not a wooded area. Within its bounds were two or three villages, chief amongst them Trawden itself, and many farms.

Colne in those days was a considerable place. Along with Burnley, Padiham, Clitheroe and Whalley it was one of the established market towns on the perimeter of Pendle Forest. All but Padiham had grammar schools and the master of the one at Colne makes a brief appearance in this chronicle of witchcraft. On the east side of the town was the area known as Colne Field and it was here, as Alizon left on the road to Trawden, that she met a pedlar—John Law, of Halifax. Potts describes him as a 'petty chapman'. These pedlars and packmen supplied many of the wants of villagers before the establishment of the regular village shops. Alizon asked him for some pins but he refused to undo his pack and she became angry with him. Sadly for her, they had scarcely parted when he had what we assume to have been a stroke. He was carried into an ale-house and as he lay there speechless, he saw Alizon, who had followed, and convinced himself that she had bewitched him.

A letter was sent from Colne to John Law's son, Abraham, in Halifax, who came straightaway to see his father. Action quickly followed. Abraham went in search of Alizon, and having found her, brought her to his father, who was presumably still in Colne. This was on 29 March. John Law, his speech by now recovered, charged the girl in the hearing of his son and others, with having bewitched him. She confessed that she had, begged his forgiveness and according to the record he gave it. But if the father forgave her the son was not prepared to let the matter rest, and on Monday, 30 March, we find Abraham Law at Read and with him were Alizon, her mother Elizabeth, and her brother James.

A name which occurs on nearly every page of Potts' chronicle is that of the magistrate to whom Abraham Law made his complaint, the man who conducted the subsequent enquiries, Roger Nowell of Read. Nowell was born in 1551, so he was now just turned sixty. He eventually died in his seventy-second year, and was buried at Whalley on 31 January 1623. He had ten children, five boys and five girls, the youngest born after 1600. Potts, who had a high opinion of Nowell, just as he seems to have had a high opinion of all his superiors, says this:

> In the end, Roger Nowell Esquire, one of his Maiesties Iustices in these partes, a very religious honest Gentleman, painefull in the seruice of his Countrey: whose fame for this great seruice . . . shall liue after him, tooke vpon him to enter into the particular examination of these suspected persons: And . . . made such a discouery of them . . . as the like hath not been heard of.

Before Nowell, Abraham Law, described as a cloth-dyer, told of his being called to Colne by the letter which reached him about 21 March. He found his father paralysed down the left side 'all save his eye', but somewhat recovered in his ability to speak, able to tell his son of the encounter on the highway near

Colne and to attribute his lameness to the work of Alizon Device, brought upon him by her witchcraft.

Alizon confessed to Nowell that she had lamed Law and described in detail what had occurred. She had, she said, wanted to buy some pins, but the pedlar had refused to undo his pack. Then there came to her a black dog which asked 'in English', 'What wouldst thou have me to do unto yonder man?' 'What canst thou do to him?' she asked. 'I can lame him,' said the dog. 'Lame him!' she said, and before the pedlar had gone two hundred yards he fell down lame. She followed into the alehouse where he was taken, then went begging to Trawden.

Nowell now had a charge against the girl, and her confession to it, but she did not stop there. She described her initiation into witchcraft and told how her grandmother had sundry times as they were out begging together tried to persuade her to let a devil or familiar 'appear unto her'. This familiar, she was promised, if allowed to suck at some part of her body, would arrange that she might have and do what she would. Eventually, about two years back, as she was walking through Roughlee, the black dog had first come to her and asked for her soul. Thus enticed, she sat down, whereupon 'the said Blacke-Dogge did with his mouth sucke at her breast, a little below her Paps, which place did remain blew halfe a yeare next after'. She then went on to recount three unconnected instances of Demdike's witchcraft.

Firstly, a local farmer, John Nutter of the Bull Hole, had a cow which was sick, and requested Demdike to 'mend' it. So at ten o'clock at night Alizon led her blind grandmother from the house and left her for half an hour, after which time Alizon's younger sister, Jennet, brought her in again. Alizon did not know what the old woman did when she was outside, but when she heard next morning that the cow had died she concluded, so she told the magistrate, that Demdike had bewitched it to death. The second occurrence concerned a piggin full of blue milk begged by Alizon and brought into the house where her grandmother was lying in bed. (A piggin is a sort of wooden pail, with one stave which acts as a handle longer than the rest.) She left the milk and went out again, and when she returned in half an hour there was a quarter of a pound of butter in it, although Demdike still lay in bed and, we are led to suppose, she had never left it. The third incident followed the quarrel with Richard Baldwin of Wheathead, and was of a much more serious nature. Soon after they had been ordered off his land Demdike again asked to be led from the house at ten o'clock at night. Alizon took her out, and again, after half an hour, Jennet brought her in. Next morning Baldwin's daughter was sick; she languished for the space of a year, then died. Alizon told Nowell that she thought her grandmother had bewitched the child to death, as she had many times heard her curse Baldwin.

Then she went on to talk about the long enmity between her grandmother and Anne Whittle (Old Chattox), giving sufficient evidence of Chattox's evil-doing for Nowell to feel justified in taking action against her. Alizon told of the theft of meal and clothes and of her father's death. She told how, about two years ago, she had been in one Anthony Nutter's house in company with Anthony's daughter, Anne. Chattox had seen them and accused them of laughing at her. She threatened to be even with one of them and within three weeks little Anne Nutter was dead, the victim, Alizon assumed, of Chattox's jealous spite.

She next spoke of a quarrel between Chattox and John Moore, a gentleman from Higham. Moore had accused the old woman of bewitching his drink—turning his ale sour! Chattox threatened to be even with him and sure enough his little son, also called John, became ill. Sometime during the period of his illness, which was eventually fatal, Alizon came upon Chattox sitting in her own garden, holding in her lap the clay image of a child. The old woman tried to cover this with her apron but the girl had seen it. She told her mother who gave her opinion that she thought it would be the 'picture' of John Moore's child.

Another time Hugh Moore of Pendle died after accusing Chattox of bewitching his cattle; but John Nutter of the Bull Hole, the same who had once requested Demdike's help for his sick cow, escaped relatively lightly. One of Chattox's daughters, Elizabeth, had begged from him a dish full of milk and had brought it to her mother who was waiting a field's breadth away. Chattox poured the milk into a can, put two sticks across the top and began the recitation of a charm, but Nutter's son 'misliking her doings' kicked the can over and spilt the milk. Next morning one of his father's cows fell sick, lay for three or four days and then died.

All this story of Alizon's was written down, later read at the trial and copied by Potts. It is because of this that the incidents starting with her encounter with John Law can be dated so precisely.

But besides questioning, search was made for the witch's mark. It is hardly likely that Alizon escaped, having admitted to suckling a familiar spirit in the shape of a dog. We know that her mother's mark was discovered from the following:

> The sayd Elizabeth Device . . . sayth, that . . . Elizabeth Sowtherns, alias Demdike, hath had a place on her left side by the space of fourty yeares, in such sort, as was to be seene at this Examinates Examination taking, at this present time.

The conditions medically called 'polymasty '—additional breasts—and 'polythely'—supernumerary nipples—are not quite so uncommon as the layman might think; but failing the discovery of one of these, any wart or sore could be interpreted as a witch's mark. The terms 'witch's mark' and 'Devil's mark' are confusing as they are often interchanged. We have followed the more general habit of using the former for the place on the witch's body from which her familiar drew his sustenance, reserving 'Devil's mark' for the stigmatum acquired by the witch when she bound herself to Satan. Despite this displaying of her mark Elizabeth was allowed to go free, as was her son James. He had made a brief statement to the effect that one Henry

23

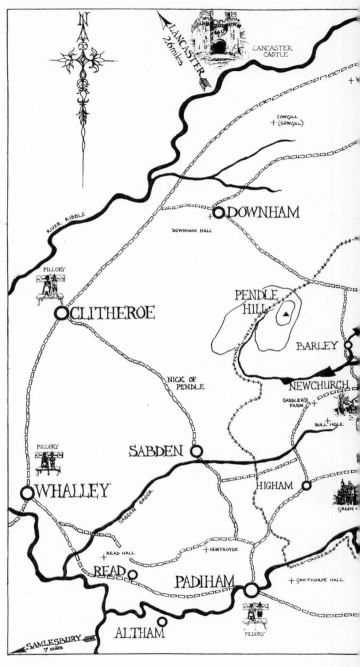

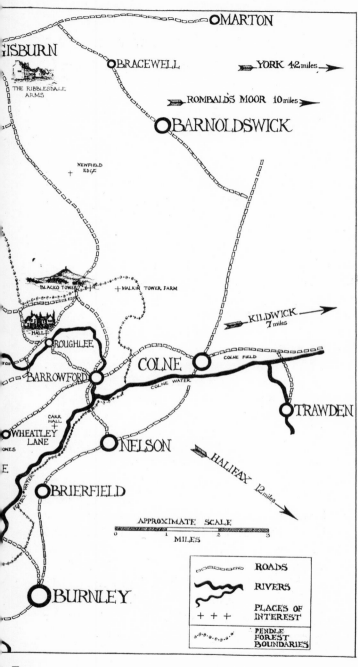

MARTON

GISBURN

THE RIBBLESDALE
ARMS

BRACEWELL

YORK 42 miles

ROMBALD'S MOOR 10 miles

BARNOLDSWICK

NEWFIELD
EDGE

BLACKO TOWER + MALKIN TOWER FARM

KILDWICK
7 miles

HALL

ROUGHLEE

COLNE

COLNE FIELD

BARROWFORD

COLNE WATER

TRAWDEN

CARR
HALL

WHEATLEY
LANE

NELSON

ONES

HALIFAX 12 miles

BRIERFIELD

APPROXIMATE SCALE

0   1   2   3
MILES

BURNLEY

ROADS

RIVERS

+ + +   PLACES OF
         INTEREST

PENDLE
FOREST
BOUNDARIES

e Forest

Bulcock had recently been to their house and accused Alizon of bewitching a child of his. She had, he said, fallen down on her knees, confessed to the crime in his hearing and begged Bulcock's forgiveness.

Alizon alone of the three Devices brought to him by Abraham Law was detained, but three days later we find the two old women and Anne Redfearn called for questioning by Nowell, along with several neighbours prepared to testify against them. The examinations on this date—2 April—took place at Fence. This village, in the middle of Pendle Forest, takes its name from the enclosure put up there in the fifteenth century to confine stags, after parts of the Forest had been let off as farms. Probably it would be easier for Nowell to ride there than to have Demdike and Chattox, with all their infirmities, taken to Read. Although everything written down on this day appears in the form of statements by those under examination, it is clear that Nowell was putting questions. He wanted details of their initiation into witchcraft and their versions of the incidents of which he had already heard, principally from Alizon.

As Demdike was to die before her trial could take place, much that was written down at Fence was never used, but Potts, whose task strictly speaking was the reporting of the proceedings at the Assizes, begs leave of his readers to be allowed to include some of the magistrate's material on Demdike, and thus be allowed to lay open the life of this 'damnable and malicious witch' whom he considered to have been the fount of all the wickedness which the cases brought to light, but who cheated the law by her untimely death. Through this we know what we do of this most famous of the Lancashire Witches, who now stood accused before Nowell.

Elizabeth Southerns (her real name), was a witch of the classic fairytale mould, old, lame and blind. She is far better known as 'Mother Demdike' or just 'Demdike'. The name is still so much on people's tongues that it is used nowadays for scooter clubs and new houses, and for a suite of rooms in

Burnley's biggest and most expensive hotel. (Another suite, naturally, is named after Chattox.) Her nickname is unexplained: it seems to have belonged to her alone, and was never used, like Chattox's, to describe any other member of her family. Nicknames, some extremely unflattering, even if honest and apt, have by no means died out in the remoter country parts of the North, and many an old man is still better known by his 'by-name' than his real one. They were almost a necessity once when, although a village might be big, surnames would be few, and around Pendle Forest particularly, the habit of using only one or two Christian names for the eldest sons of families was very prevalent. For generations the Nowells used only Roger, and for the Nutters of Greenhead we find the leap-frogging sequence, Robert–Christopher–Robert. It is almost certain that unless some descriptive nickname was used, Robert's son would be called 'Chris o' Bob's' and his son 'Bob o' Chris's' or even 'Bob o' Chris o' Bob's'.

Potts never saw Demdike, but says this about her:

> She was a very old woman, about the age of Foure-score yeares, and had been a Witch for fiftie yeares. Shee dwelt in the Forrest of Pendle, a vaste place, fitte for her profession: . . . Shee was a generall agent for the Deuill in all these partes . . . from this Sincke of villanie and mischiefe, haue all the rest proceeded.

He says she had been a witch for fifty years, her daughter said forty, and she herself admitted to twenty. Concerning the length of her years of servitude Potts comments: 'The Deuill and shee knew best with whome shee made her couenant.' She was a widow but we hear nothing of her husband, not even his name. The fact that one of her sons was called Howgate, while the family name was Southerns, suggests that he was illegitimate, unless the old woman had been married more than once.

Whether her confession was the result of threats, ill-treatment, or promises of favour, we do not know. Nowell may have convinced her that she was a witch, and that the animals she met in the fields or that strayed into her house were the Devil in disguise. Or by questions and suggestions he may have turned whatever story she told into the tale he wanted to hear, knowing that a later denial would carry little weight. Many ridiculous confessions similar to Demdike's came from people who were liable to forfeit their lives by their admissions, a fact impossible to explain satisfactorily. Torture was never allowed by English law and in the known instances where, even in England, suspects were trussed like chickens, kept awake for days or 'walked' up and down until they were ready to drop, those responsible for these practices were the self-appointed witch-finders, not magistrates or courts. We have no ground for imputing to Roger Nowell some of the tricks and stratagems illegally used by others.

Whatever persuaded her to do it, Demdike told Nowell that about twenty years ago, as she came home from begging, she met, near a stonepit in Goldshaw (one of the divisions or 'booths' in Pendle Forest), the Devil in the shape of a boy, half his coat black, half brown. In return for his promise that she should have anything she requested, she agreed to give him her soul. He said his name was Tibb, and very versatile he turned out to be, subsequently appearing as a brown dog, a black cat, and a hare. Her ageing memory recalled an incident when, on a Sunday morning, as she sat dozing with a child on her knee, a dog came into the house and, as dogs will, nuzzled against her. This was turned, whether by her or Nowell, into a visit from Tibb. He had come to suck blood under her left arm, the place in fact where her daughter three days earlier had told Nowell that Demdike had a mark. Tibb's visit, so she said, left her stark mad for eight weeks. She also admitted her inability on this occasion to invoke the name of Jesus to protect herself, an admission very much in keeping with the popularly held belief that a witch was unable to recite the Lord's Prayer. She was, however, able to say, 'Jesus save my child'.

From the trivial, but most likely factual, details which are interspersed with the fantasies of the confessions, we get interesting glimpses of the primitive and poverty-stricken life at Malkin Tower. On this Sunday morning Demdike said she was 'without any apparel saving her smock'. She next gave her own version of the killing of Baldwin's child—a version which differed in many details from her granddaughter's. She gave the time of the quarrel at the mill as 'a little before last Christmas', then went on to say that as she and Alizon were leaving, Tibb appeared and suggested revenge, to which suggestion Demdike gave her consent, telling him to get revenge on the miller or his family. Tibb then vanished out of her sight and she never saw him again. The use of the words 'appeared', 'vanished out of her sight' and 'never saw him since' must strike us as odd for a woman described on the very same page as blind! Alizon, who had dated the incident as two years previously, had made no mention of Tibb but had told of her grandmother cursing Baldwin on sundry occasions and 'praying' for him 'still and loud'.

Demdike went on to give Nowell details of the 'speediest way to take a man's life away by Witchcraft':

> Make a Picture of Clay, like vnto the shape of the person whom they meane to kill, and dry it thorowly: and when they would haue them to be ill in any one place more than an other; then take a Thorne or Pinne, and pricke it in that part of the Picture you would so haue to be ill: and when you would haue any part of the Body to consume away, then take that part of the Picture, and burne it. And when they would haue the whole body to consume away, then take the remnant of the sayd Picture, and burne it: and so therevpon by that meanes, the body shall die.

The technique which Demdike described is very ancient. Mention of it is found in the histories of ancient Chaldea, Egypt, Greece and Rome. In Egypt the images, of wax or clay, were often cursed, bound as if dead, or stuck with pins or miniature weapons. These figures may at one time have been the means of concentrating hypnotic power, but as the witches now used them they were probably a straightforward example of sympathetic magic—harm to the image to harm the man. They are undoubtedly still used in less civilised societies, and still, on occasions, desperately tried in more sophisticated ones.

Following this confession of her own depravity Demdike went on to talk of Chattox. She described a visit to Redfearn's house shortly before Robert Nutter's death, when she had caught Chattox and her daughter Anne sitting outside by the ditch making three pictures of clay. Demdike's familiar, Tibb, in the shape of a black cat on this occasion, had told her on enquiry that they were the pictures of Christopher Nutter, Robert Nutter and Robert's wife, Marie. Tibb suggested that Demdike might help them fashion the pictures and when she declined he pushed her angrily into the ditch and so spilt the milk she was carrying.

After Demdike, Chattox herself was examined. Whatever the pathetic old creature said, Nowell was able to write down as her 'voluntary confession' the statement that fourteen or fifteen years ago 'a thing like a Christian man' had pestered her for four years to give him her soul. Eventually, in her own house, she had consented and was promised that from thenceforward she would want for nothing and be avenged on whom she would. She was told to call her spirit 'Fancie' and he promised to be ready whenever she summoned him. Very soon Fancie, seemingly wearied of inactivity, was urging her to harm the wife of Richard Baldwin, and when she refused to comply he tried to bite her arm.

On the subject of the deaths of the two Nutters, father and son, eighteen or nineteen years previously, Chattox maintained that young Robert's grandmother, Elizabeth, had first approached her, and two other women now dead, with a request that they should bring about the young man's death. This was in order that the land destined for him should be inherited by 'the Women—their Coosens'. The other two women approached, both of Burnley, were named as Jane Boothman and Loomeshaw's wife. The three consented, but Chattox's son-in-law,

Thomas Redfearn, who seems from the little we hear of him to have been a peace-loving man, intervened, and talked Chattox off the project. Loomeshaw's wife would have killed him for this, but she was 'stayed by the learning' of one Baldwyn, late schoolmaster at Colne, who was rewarded for this by Redfearn with the present of a capon.

The old woman then gave a new slant on young Robert Nutter, whose urgent requests concerning the Chattoxes his father had chosen to ignore. Anne Redfearn must have had a certain charm in those far-off days because, according to her mother, Robert went to Redfearn's house to 'have his pleasure of her'. Landlord or no Anne resisted and Robert rode off in a rage, threatening that if ever the ground came to him they should be turned off it. Chattox confessed that following this attempt to seduce her daughter she called Fancie to her and bade him take revenge on Robert. She said no more than that, except to add that in her opinion Loomeshaw's wife and Jane Boothman were as much accountable for his death as she herself.

Margaret Crook, Robert Nutter's sister, was present at Fence on 2 April. She spoke briefly, but without giving the reason, of her brother's quarrel with Anne Redfearn and of his repeated assertions, following the quarrel, that Anne had bewitched him. Next, John Nutter told Nowell of the journey home from Burnley, those eighteen or nineteen years before, with his brother and father; and one James Robinson, who about that time had lived at Greenhead, possibly as a servant, gave evidence that Chattox and Anne Redfearn were commonly reputed to be witches. This had evidently not stopped his wife, about six years before the enquiry, from hiring the old woman to card wool in their house. Unfortunately Chattox had dipped a cup into some new casks of drink and soured the lot. She was unable to right it, although she claimed to have a charm for the mending of drink that was 'forespoken or bewitched'; Nowell assiduously wrote it down:

31

Three Biters hast thou bitten,
The Hart, ill Eye, ill Tonge:
Three bitter shall be thy Boote
Father, Sonne, and Holy Ghost
a Gods name.
Fiue Pater-nosters, fiue Auies,
and a Creede,
In worship of fiue wounds
of our Lord.

She had once, she said, successfully used this at the request of
John Moore's wife and when, despite her putting the drink to
rights, Moore's wife had chided her, she called on Fancie who
bit one of Moore's cows on the head, in consequence of which
it went mad and died. On 30 March Alizon, in describing the
same incident, had made no mention of the ale being restored
and had said it was Moore's child who had died. Yet again did
Chattox, in place of Alizon's accusations of murdered children,
try to substitute victims less worthy of concern. She admitted
to killing another cow, the property of Anthony Nutter, whereas
Alizon has spoken of his daughter Anne dying. In explaining
this crime the old woman confirmed the rivalry reported to exist between her family and Old Demdike's. She said that: 'She
perceived Anthony Nutter of Pendle to favour Elizabeth
Southerns, alias Demdike.' Whereupon, she admitted, she summoned Fancie and told him to kill Nutter's cow.

The two old women had now confessed to being witches, to
having familiar spirits, and to making use of these for their evil
ends. Anne Redfearn said nothing, or if she did it was not recorded, but the evidence of the others was considered sufficient
proof against her. As a justice of the peace Nowell now had,
like his present-day counterparts, to make up his mind whether
to deal with the cases summarily, or to send the accused to a
higher court for trial. Considering the confessions, the gravity
of the charges against them, and the severe Witchcraft Act then
in force, it is not surprising that he decided to detain Demdike,
Chattox and Anne Redfearn whilst arranging for their

dispatch, along with Alizon Device, to Lancaster for the Assizes.

The laws and the times were different then, and while today a JP makes a decision purely on the evidence presented to him, usually by the police, Nowell had been quite within his rights to examine the prisoners inquisitorially, actively searching for evidence and in fact getting up the case against them himself. There was, in fact, a positive incentive for zealous magistrates to go witch-hunting: the known and published opinions of their king! It will help to explain Nowell's actions if we know what those opinions were.

In 1612, James I and VI was on the English throne. In 1604, the first year of his English reign, the act under which the Lancashire Witches were tried had been passed. James, 'the wisest fool in Christendom' and a man of first-class intellect, imagined that his eminence, the knowledge he had accumulated after years of study, and his personal acquaintance with witches, had made him a particularly prominent target for the Devil. In general he regarded it as presumptuous for any of his subjects to question his 'divine right' to do as he liked and although he was stoutly resisted when his actions threatened the welfare of landlords and merchants, few people were prepared to oppose him on behalf of the poor wretches hanged as witches. His studies and writings on the subject were considered to have made him an authority.

In Scotland he used to attend witch trials, and at one of these, angered by the acquittal of one Barbara Napier, the king went so far as to charge the jury with an 'Assize of Error' and have the perverse jurors arrested. They agreed to submit to the king's will and James' explanation for his interference in the case was put into print and published. The jury had acquitted Barbara, a woman of good standing, incidentally, because the only evidence against her had come from the other accused, and had been forced from them by torture. James explained to them:

c   33

By the Civil law I know that such persons are not received as witnesses, but in the matters of heresy [and] matters of witchcraft [there is] good reason that they be admitted. First none honest can know these matters, second, because they will not accuse themselves, thirdly, because no act that is done by them can be seen.

James applied himself to the study of witchcraft and as the culmination of his work, in 1597, his *Demonology* was published in Edinburgh. There was at the time a suggestion in some quarters that it was not really his own writing, but it seems to have been generally accepted as such and to have had the influence one would expect with so eminent an author. It is rather tiresome reading, being in the form of a dialogue, one person feeding questions to the other, but as witch books go it is reasonably short and can be taken as representing ideas on the subject current in the early seventeenth century. Significantly, in 1602, before James came to the English throne, it was already being quoted in a Dorset witch trial, and although mentioned only once by name in the trial at Lancaster in 1612, it clearly had a bearing on the case. A justice of the peace such as Nowell was probably as bewildered as the accused when first required to assess accusations of witchcraft. *Demonology* was the sort of book, in fact the most likely book, to which he would refer for guidance.

'I call them witches which do renounce God and yield themselves wholly to the Devil,' James wrote. Witches were designated 'slaves of the Devil'—the instruments through whom the assaults of Satan were practised. They therefore merited severe punishment. Satan supplied them with familiar spirits who could be ordered to bring them all sorts of dainty dishes, and his contract with them specified the fashion which the familiar would assume when they called him. 'Usually,' he explained, 'the familiar shows unto them in the likeness of a dog, a cat, an ape, or suchlike beast.' As for the reasons for seeking to become witches, those who were poverty-stricken and miserable were

34

tempted by the lure of rich food and wealth, whereas the well-to-do were drawn by thoughts of power and the promise of satisfying a desperate desire for revenge against their enemies. The steps to initiation were enumerated. The Devil first introduced himself, always when they were alone, walking solitary in the fields perhaps, or lying in bed. In the guise of a man, or perhaps as a disembodied voice, he enquired what troubled them, and promised a sudden and certain remedy. At the next meeting, if he could persuade them to renounce God and their baptism and addict themselves to his service, he gave them his mark. It was explained why there were more women witches than men. They were the frailer sex and therefore more easily ensnared. James then described how the Devil caused them to convene in great numbers for his service, and how he taught them, at their convening, how to work all kinds of mischief. He showed them how to make 'pictures' of wax or clay, so that by the crumbling thereof victims could be wasted by continual sickness. They were taught other ways to cause and cure disease, how to make love potions, 'joynt' (ie dismember) corpses, and make powders therefrom, and how to raise storms and tempests. Witches, we are told, 'conversed naturally', ie had carnal intercourse, 'with incubi and succubi'. But never must evil be allowed to pay dividends, and the reader is assured that such intercourse was extremely painful, at least to women, as amongst other abnormalities the Devil's sperm was as cold as ice.

James put forward two helpful suggestions for discovering the witches' guilt: 'One was the finding of their mark, and the trying the insensibleness thereof.'

Just as none who are not marked with God's mark can meet to adore him, so none not marked with the Devil's mark can. He gives them his mark, upon some secret place of their body, which remains sore unhealed until his next meeting with them, and thereafter ever insensible—however it be nipped or pricked!

35

James was copying continental opinion, which averred that the most likely place to find the Devil's mark on women was on the breasts or private parts, and the king's earnest advice was taken as sanction for many repellent practices in Scotland and to a lesser extent England. Women were stripped, hair was shaved or even pulled out and, if no mark could be clearly discerned, a needle was stuck into the flesh until some insensitive place was discovered.

Nowell cannot be charged with having tried this test, but not many years after, in Newcastle-on-Tyne, a Scot was able to charge a sovereign a head for his services as an experienced 'pricker'. The bellman was sent round the town to invite any that had complaint against any woman to have her sent to the Town Hall for examination. Confronted by a good-looking young woman this man 'in sight of all the people', laid her body naked to the waist with her clothes over her head. Then he began to run a pin into her thigh. Another Scots 'pricker' who had been apprehended for other villainies confessed that the whole procedure was a fraud. By pretending to prick or by using an instrument where the point slid back into the handle a dishonest man could declare that he had found the morbid spot which indicated a witch.

James also recommended their 'fleeting' on the water, which could refuse to receive them 'on her bosom'. Witches were not just tossed into a pond or dammed-up stream. Customarily the left hand and right foot were bound together, the other hand and foot likewise. Despite the obvious risk of drowning if the water did accept them and they sank, there were many cases of suspected women asking to be 'swum', in other words given the ancient and now royally recommended privilege of trial by ordeal. There is nothing to show that any of the Lancashire Witches underwent this rough and fallible test.

How, it may be wondered, did anyone whose business it was to enforce the law against such monsters dare to act? James had the answer: '. . . if the magistrate will be diligent in examining

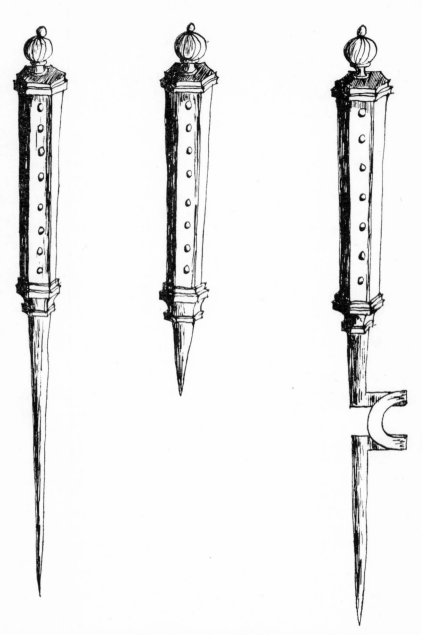

Witchfinders' bodkins. The centre bodkin has a retractable point

them, God will not permit their master to trouble and hinder so good a work. If he be slothful toward them, God is very able to make them instruments to waken and punish his sloth.' And why, with the powers attributed to them, did any witch suffer herself to be imprisoned and tried, when she could presumably have slipped her chains and transported herself, as she did to the sabbat, through doors and up chimneys, past any bolts and bars? According to James: 'When the witches are apprehended and detained by the lawful magistrates, their power is then no greater than before that ever they meddled with these matters.' Finally, on the disposal of condemned witches the king wrote: '. . . they should be consumed by fire—yet in every country according to the law and custom thereof, but regardless of sex, age or rank. Bairns, because of their less and ignorant age, might be excused.'

However, even after the Union and removal of James to London, the two countries continued to deal with witches after their own fashions. England to its credit, alone amongst the countries of Western Europe, did not permit witches to be tortured; unless they had committed treason they were straightforwardly sentenced to be 'hanged until dead'. Scotland followed the continental example with torture and the stake, and the margin of many an old Scottish Court Book bears the melancholy record written in after trial 'Convicta et combusta'.

Much of what Nowell was able to set down as voluntary confession bore out what James had written, which suggests that the magistrate was asking a series of questions designed to get his prisoners to admit to a pattern of behaviour which fitted with the definition of witches as supplied by books such as *Demonology*.

The statements of Demdike, Chattox and Alizon Device are in much the same mould. They all told of their early meetings with their 'spirits' and all the women admitted that they had given him a place somewhere about the breasts, where he could 'suck'. They all told of various occasions when their spirits had appeared to them, said where they had seen them, what form

38

they were in, and the purpose of the meeting. And in the crimes to which they admitted the pattern was always the same. They had a motive for disliking someone. Their familiar suggested that they should do him harm. He was then either instructed to do it, or he taught them the method by which it could be done, usually by making pictures of clay. However, it will never be known how Nowell obtained these confessions and the fact that the accused admitted to the manifestly impossible throws doubt on everything they said, and on the means by which the confessions were obtained.

Those questioned would undoubtedly believe in witches themselves. Did Nowell perhaps persuade them that they had indeed been witches for years? This might have shocked them but would they be more unbelieving than we would be if told by a doctor that we were typhoid carriers, or had been unknowingly harbouring the germs of tuberculosis? In times when one child in three could be expected to die before reaching the age of five, and when little was understood about hygiene or infection, commonplace ailments and everyday accidents, as well as fatal illnesses to cattle and children, were ascribed to the workings of demons or witches. If a seventeenth-century man could have been presented with modern knowledge of the causes of illness, what explanation would he have been likely to find more reasonable, that maladies and deaths were caused by a variety of things called germs, viruses or microbes, so small as to be invisible, or that they were brought on by the will of man or woman, visible, powerful and intelligent, operating in collusion with evil spirits? Were evil spirits not taught of in scripture and believed in by Jesus himself, who had indeed claimed to drive them out?

Were they promised leniency, or made to think that others had already told everything there was to know about them? Ignorant of the law, did they think that confession and cooperation with authority would be to their advantage? Although in at least one English trial liberal promises of mercy were

39

given and then unscrupulously broken when confessions had been obtained, conviction of accused witches was not as automatic in England as it became in the rest of Europe. There were women in the Lancashire Witches' own district who had been charged and acquitted. On the very day, 4 April, when the four left for Lancaster, one who was a few weeks later to figure in Pendle witchcraft was beginning her journey home from York a free woman.

The committal to Lancaster of the four women might have marked the end of Nowell's loyal enquiries but, to quote Potts,

heere they had not stayed a weeke, when their Children and Friendes being abroad at libertie, laboured a speciall meeting at Malking Tower . . . vpon Good-fryday . . . of all the most dangerous, wicked and damnable Witches in the County farre and neere.

This meeting is often instanced as the only recorded example of a witches' sabbat in England at that time. Compared with the satanic midnight orgies reputedly taking place on the Continent, this noon gathering, consisting mostly of worried and helpless peasants, was a tame affair. They were unable to depend on the Devil to find them something to eat, and their hunger was appeased by a meal of beef, bacon and mutton, the last from a sheep stolen the night before by James Device. Their meeting was not a secret for long; notice of it came to Nowell and he resumed his investigations. Not necessarily in person! What he, as a justice of the peace, decreed should be done, it was the unpopular duty of the constable to do. The office of constable was a yearly appointment running from Michaelmas to the following Michaelmas. It was unpaid but the serving of it was obligatory. The constable's duties included the apprehension and escorting of criminals, including witches, to the Assizes. Henry Hargreaves, yeoman, held the office for Pendle Forest, and sometime between Good Friday, 10 April, and Monday 27 April, he visited Malkin Tower and, with the help of James Device unearthed, a few yards outside the wall, a clay image and some teeth—the latter from the graveyard at Newchurch. He also during this time took James over to Gisburn, a few miles away in Yorkshire, to identify Jennet Preston—the woman acquitted at York at the Lent Assizes and now once again accused and known to have been to the meeting at Malkin Tower. Then, on 27 April, Nowell called in the help of another magistrate, Nicholas Bannister, of Altham, and at the house of one James Wilsey, in Pendle Forest, they examined Elizabeth, James and Jennet Device, principally on the subject of the Good Friday meeting.

Jennet Device was nine! Nowell had already heard of her: it was she who had been sent to fetch her grandmother indoors on the two occasions Alizon had told of, when Old Demdike had wished to be left alone outside to work her magic. He must have realised that he had a godsend in Jennet, only a child, yet acceptable as a witness against the exceptional crime of witchcraft, and not herself accused. As Potts revealingly says: 'by his great paines taken in the Examination of Iennet Deuice, al their practises are now made knowen.' She first told how the sheep for their feast had been stolen by her brother from a Barley farmer, and how he had brought it home and killed it in the house while she watched. She gave the number present at Malkin Tower as about twenty, all witches, her mother had told her. She could name only six, but James was able to give a much longer list. He missed out one of the men mentioned by his sister and when Potts tabulated the names for his readers' benefit he carelessly omitted several people who were obviously there. By joining all three lists it seems that these were the people at Malkin Tower assembled for what Potts called 'the Great Assembly and Feast':

Elizabeth Device, daughter of Old Demdike, whose house it now was;
James Device, son of Elizabeth, who provided the mutton;
Jennet Device, nine-year-old sister to James, who later played a very important role in the trial;

41

Christopher Howgate (or Holgate) of Pendle, Demdike's son; Elizabeth Howgate, his wife;

Jennet Hargreaves, wife of Hugh Hargreaves, of Under Pendle, a farm on the Pendle Hill side of Barley;

Alice Nutter: Jennet Device described her as Dick Myles wife, of Roughlee; James spoke of the mother of Myles Nutter;

Christopher Hargreaves (nicknamed Christopher Jackes) of Thorneyholme;

Elizabeth Hargreaves, his wife;

John Bulcock, of Moss End, a farm near Newchurch;

Jane Bulcock, his mother;

Alice Gray, of Colne;

Katherine Hewitt, of Colne, nicknamed Mouldheels;

Ann Cronkshaw of Marsden;

Grace Hay of Padiham;

Jennet Preston, of Gisburn in Craven, newly released after her trial at York.

Also two women from Burnley, whose names are not given, and according to Potts 'many more, which being bound ouer to appeare at the last Assizes, are since that time fled to saue themselues'.

The business of the meeting as described to Nowell had been threefold. First, they planned to blow up Lancaster Castle, murder the gaoler and bring about the release of the four women imprisoned there. If these were indeed their intentions it displays their low mentality, as Lancaster Castle is a considerable fortress. Some of them had probably seen it—it was the custom for thousands, from as much as forty miles away, to make regularly the trek to Lancaster to witness the hangings that invariably followed the Assizes. Secondly, they had met to give a name to Alizon Device's spirit (she was a relatively new recruit to witchcraft). As she was not there they could not perform this ceremony. Thirdly, they promised to help Jennet Preston of Gisburn, in her feud with the Listers of that place. They were the family responsible for Jennet's arrest and recent trial.

The whole of the evidence about the supposed business of this meeting is suspect, coming as it did from a little girl and her evidently half-witted brother, James. It is more likely that those present, mostly relatives or near neighbours, were drawn together by rumours that they had been implicated in the confessions of the four now at Lancaster. The long statement by James is a fine example of the inexplicable nonsense offered as evidence by this young man, or put into his mouth by the magistrates. Two years previously, he said, on Shere Thursday (the day before Easter, now better known as Maundy Thursday), his grandmother had sent him to church to receive communion, telling him not to eat the bread which the minister gave him but to deliver it 'to such a thing as should meet him on his way homewards'. The thing turned out to be a hare, which threatened to pull him to pieces when it found that James had perversely eaten the bread. He saved himself from harm by 'marking himself to God'—crossing himself, whereupon the hare vanished. When approached near Newchurch some four days after this incident, by a brown dog which requested his soul, James replied that it was not his to give, but his saviour Jesus Christ's. This dog pestered him again on sundry occasions, each time earnestly requesting his soul in exchange for the power to revenge himself on whom he would. But James would only agree to giving up that part of his soul which he considered belonged to him.

In another part of his statement we reach rock-bottom for nonsense and triviality; Nowell and Bannister nevertheless thought it worth while to have written down as significant what he said: 'About a month agoe, [he] mette a browne Dogge coming from his Graund-mothers house, two or three nights after [he] heard a voyce of a great number of Children screiking and crying pittifully, about day-light gate.' [This, sometimes shortened to 'daygate', is an old and rather attractive expression for sunset.] Some days later, soon after daybreak, he heard 'a foule yelling like vnto a great number of Cattes' and three nights after that, at midnight appropriately, there came a thing 'coloured blacke, and about the bignesse of a Hare or Catte, and lay vpon him very heauily about an houre, and went then from him out of his Chamber window.'

Hares seem to have been something of a menace to James. They threatened to pull him to pieces, lay heavily upon him at night, and another time, when he was on his way home from Chattox's house, one of them spat fire at him! He told how he eventually acquired a spirit in the shape of a dog which he was told to call Dandie, and on the last occasion Dandie had been with him, on the Tuesday before he was apprehended, he described it as vanishing like a pantomime demon 'with a most fearful cry and yell and a great flash of fire'. He explained the teeth found at his mother's house:

> Twelue yeares agoe, Anne Chattox, at a Buriall at the new Church in Pendle, did take three scalpes of people, which had been buried and then cast out of a graue . . . and tooke eight teeth out of the said Scalpes, whereof she kept foure to herselfe, and gaue other foure to the said Demdike . . . which said teeth haue euer since beene kept, vntill now found by . . . Henry Hargreues and this Examinate, at the West-end of this Examinates Grand-mothers house, and there buried in the earth, and a Picture of Clay there likewise found by them, about halfe a yard ouer in the earth.

This macabre example of co-operation between the two old women is in contrast to the other tales of jealousy, theft, fear and bribery. Altogether a very confusing picture emerges of the relationship between the two families.

As against this trivia James admitted to two murders. A Mistress Towneley of Carr Hall had come upon him in her kitchen, perhaps on one of his begging expeditions. She accused him and his mother of stealing turves (peat for the fire), and sent him packing with a slap between the shoulders. Dandie came to him a day or two later and helped in the fashioning of a clay picture. James dried it by the fire the same night, crumbled it piecemeal for a week, and two days later Anne Towneley was dead! One John Duckworth had promised him an old shirt, and then refused it. Dandie met James again and the supposed conversation between the lad and his canine familiar is interesting as it brings in the primitive belief that power over another person is heightened by possessing something of his, or by having touched him. Dandie said: 'Thou didst touch the said Duckworth.' James denied this, but his familiar knew better. 'Yes,' said Dandie, 'thou didst touch him, therefore I haue power of him.' Duckworth was dead within a week; there is no mention of a clay 'picture' in this case.

James said much to incriminate his mother, describing in some detail how she and her familiar spirit had done away with a local farmer, John Robinson, alias Swyer, of Barley. Ball, Elizabeth's familiar, had instructed his mother to make a picture of clay in the likeness of Robinson, dry it hard, then crumble it little by little. Next day her son watched Elizabeth fashioning the clay. She brought it into the house where it took two days to dry. Then for three weeks she slowly crumbled it. Two days after the final destruction of his image John Robinson died.

By the time Elizabeth Device came before him Nowell was able to confront her with the accusations of her children. Potts says:

> Vpon her Examination . . . she would confess nothing, vntill . . . knowing, that both Iennet Deuice, her daughter [and] Iames Deuice, her sonne, had accused her and layed open all things, in their Examinations . . . she made a very liberall and voluntarie Confession.

She agreed on the names of those at Malkin Tower, as previously disclosed by James. She agreed also that they had met, pointlessly as it befell, to name her daughter's spirit and to give help to Jennet Preston, but she denied hearing of any plot to blow up Lancaster Castle and kill the gaoler. She acknowledged the responsibility for killing John Robinson, giving as her reason that he had accused her of having had a bastard child 'by one Sellar'. She admitted also to having brought about the

45

death of Robinson's brother, James. No reason was given for this but her spirit Ball had helped.

Jennet and James, in reporting so freely what they had heard and seen on Good Friday, had not only thoroughly implicated their mother but in telling who was at the meeting they involved many others outside the family. However, whether because they were the only suspects he could catch, or because there was insufficient evidence against the others, from the twenty or so reported present at Malkin Tower by the Devices only Alice Nutter of Roughlee, John and Jane Bulcock of Moss End, Katherine Hewitt and Alice Gray of Colne were rounded up and sent, with James and his mother, to join Demdike, Chattox, Anne Redfearn and Alizon Device in the Castle at Lancaster. The evidence against them was slight and as it was read out or repeated when the time came for them to be tried, it can be kept until then. There were now eleven in all from Pendle or thereabouts sent by Roger Nowell to await their trials for witchcraft, all housed in a dungeon in the Castle's Well Tower. In charge of them and the whole prison part of the building was Thomas Covell: it will be remembered that one of the items of business at Malkin Tower on Good Friday was to arrange for his early death. Gaols and gaolers in the seventeenth century had little in common with prisons and prison governors today. The idea of detaining criminals as a punishment was only just taking hold, and the cells and dungeons were then used principally as secure places in which people could be kept to await the next Assizes. Condemned criminals were either hanged, outlawed, mutilated or sentenced to exposure in the pillory, leaving the gaol temporarily almost clear. 'Whipped next Market Day', 'Branded in the shoulder', 'Placed in the pillory', are typical entries, written in, after sentence, against the names of prisoners.

Old Demdike had survived the journey to the gaol but soon died. The date of her death is not known but as her companion in the cell, Old Chattox, was again examined at Lancaster on

19 May and there is no mention of Demdike being so examined, it seems likely that she had died by this date. This likelihood is further strengthened when we notice the change between Chattox's confession of 2 April, and this one, in the prison, in May. At Fence she had admitted to being a witch for fourteen or fifteen years, but never suggested that Demdike had persuaded her to become one. The only time she mentioned her was merely to suggest that there was some rivalry between them. At Lancaster she put the blame for her conversion emphatically on to Old Demdike through whose 'wicked perswasions and counsell [she] was seduced to condescend & agree to become subiect vnto that deuelish abhominable profession of Witchcraft'.

She also altered the place of her final conversion from her own home to Malkin Tower, and described an unsatisfying meal of flesh, butter, cheese, bread and drink served to the two women by their spirits, Tibb and Fancie. She mentioned other things about which she seems to have kept silent before. Whilst describing her first meeting with her familiar, she owned to having given him a place 'on her right side near her ribs' to suck upon. She also said she had heard Demdike confess to the murder by witchcraft of Richard Assheton of Downham, and to a share in the killing of Robert Nutter of Greenhead, the latter crime in conjunction with herself and Widow Loomeshaw of Burnley. Jane Boothman previously mentioned in connection with this crime had seemingly been forgotten.

This examination was conducted by Thomas Covell, here described as 'one of his majesty's coroners'. With him were the mayor of Lancaster, William Sandes, and a justice of the peace, James Anderton, of Clayton, near Lancaster. James Device was also examined by these three on the same day as Chattox. He said nothing new but repeated the assertion that he had consented to yield up only a part of his soul, that which he considered was his to bestow, the rest being kept for his maker. A possible explanation for why these two of all the accused were again examined could have been their state of health. If Demdike had died, Chattox's chances of surviving a further three months in the cell must have been questionable. Perhaps James's condition was giving cause for concern; as we shall read when the time came for him to face the court he was, of all the prisoners, in the most pitiable state.

CHAPTER III

August 1612—The Assizes at Lancaster

In the squalor of that Lancaster dungeon, the men and women arrested on Roger Nowell's orders spent the early summer of 1612. They were joined by other suspected witches. A woman from Padiham was sent by Nicholas Bannister, who had sat with Nowell at the big enquiry on 27 April. Another came from near St Helens, and three women came from Samlesbury, a village between Blackburn and Preston. Of four others—two men and two women—called Samlesbury Witches, we know very little, as their trials were not reported. These made up the 'nineteene notorious witches' advertised on the title-page of Potts' book, and of this number our principal interest is in the Pendle Forest group consisting of:

> Anne Whittle, alias Chattox
> Elizabeth Device
> James Device
> Anne Redfearn
> Alice Nutter
> Katherine Hewitt
> John Bulcock
> Jane Bulcock
> Alizon Device

The balance is made up by:

Margaret Pearson of Padiham
Isobel Roby, of Windle, near St Helens

Jennet Bierley Ellen Bierley Jane Southworth John Ramsden Elizabeth Astley Alice Gray Isabel Sidegraves Lawrence Haye	All listed by Potts as the Samlesbury Witches, although Alice Gray should belong to the Pendle group, and only the trials of Jane Bierley, Ellen Bierley and Jane Southworth are reported.

The law under which the Lancashire Witches were to be tried was the most severe of a succession of Witchcraft Acts traceable back over the centuries. Witchcraft had been mentioned in laws passed by both Church and State since very early times, but the interpretation of the word was different then and what was called witchcraft would have been better defined as sorcery. Sorcerers used spells and charms, and were believed to be helped by spirits. They had recourse to incantations, wax images and heads of corpses in attempts to master the powers of the unseen world, but the definite pact with the Devil, so integral a feature of later witchcraft, was not charged against them. Under early laws it seems that sorcerers were tried by the same procedures as anyone else, and were punished not for their attempts to use magic, but for the actual harm they did thereby. If some tangible crime could be proved against them then punishment followed—perhaps only a period of penance or fasting. Ineffectual practitioners of the black arts, no matter what was found in their possession by way of skulls, severed heads, wax effigies, or books of magic, were leniently dealt with if they promised to mend their ways.

Trial procedures as we would expect differed in many respects from those of today. Sorcerers, as well as others, could, for instance, claim the privilege of trial by ordeal, a practice founded on the belief that God would actively interpose to see justice done. It is on record that in the reign of King John, one Gideon, who was accused of sorcery by Agnes, the wife of Odo the merchant was acquitted 'by the judgment of iron'. This picking up of a pound of hot iron was one common ordeal;

others were the plucking of a stone out of boiling water, or being 'swum'—thrown bodily into a pond or river, where sinking denoted innocence, inability to sink showing guilt. Although the right to be tried by these crude methods was abolished as early as 1219, the practice of 'swimming' witches survived, and was as we have read commended by James I. He explained that as witches had renounced their Christian baptism it was to be expected that water, the element used to perform the holy rite, should reject them.

The first of the modern English laws against witchcraft was passed in 1542, towards the end of the reign of Henry VIII. The conception of witchcraft was still different from that across the Channel, and the nearest the Act came to mentioning a covenant with the Devil was to speak of the 'loss of the souls of such offenders to the great dishonour of God'. This Act made witchcraft a criminal offence. Before this it had been dealt with by Ecclesiastical Courts. The power which these courts and the clergy generally at one time had is little realised today: it is well described in Chaucer's *Friar's Tale*:

> In my own district once there used to be
> A fine archdeacon, one of high degree,
> Who boldly did the execution due
> On fornication and on witchcraft too,
> Bawdry, adultery and defamation,
> Breaches of wills and contracts, spoliation
> Of church endowments, failure in the rents
> And tithes and disregard of sacraments,
> All these and many other kinds of crime
> That need have no rehearsal at this time
> . . .
> And he had jurisdiction, on inspection,
> And powers to administer correction.

As the dominance of the Church grew less, and as more and more offences were brought within the bounds of Common Law, the influence of the Church Courts dwindled and today they are almost solely concerned with clergy discipline.

The Witchcraft Act of 1542 was repealed in 1547 and there is no record of anyone being made to suffer its prescribed penalties, but in 1563 the Convocation of the Church of England pleaded that 'there be some penal, yea, capital pains for witches and sorcerers'. Active in this call for renewed legislation were members of the clergy, some of them now bishops, who had been driven out of England during the reign of Mary, had found refuge on the Continent, and had seemingly absorbed some of the fashionable witchcraft beliefs from there. So, in that year, 1563, the fifth of Elizabeth's reign, a law was passed which was more or less a copy of the repealed Act of sixteen years before. In it, death was the penalty for murder by witchcraft, and for a second conviction of causing bodily injury. Property was also confiscated for a second conviction for destruction of goods or the procuring of unlawful love. Exposure in the pillory and a year's imprisonment were prescribed for some of the less serious offences. Elizabeth's Act marked the beginning of English witch-hunting, which remained sporadic, however, for the whole of its continuance. Outbursts coincided with the presence of a zealous magistrate, a self-appointed witch-finder, or a malicious child, to whose accusations someone was prepared to give ear. Before Elizabeth died, over five hundred people had been indicted for witchcraft, but only about a fifth of these were hanged—a remarkably low fraction when one considers the almost automatic burnings on the Continent.

The main area of persecution was South East England, where the first important trial was staged, at Chelmsford, in 1566, three years after the passing of the Act. Only three women were concerned, and only one, Agnes Waterhouse, was hanged, on 29 July. She can be considered the first victim of English witchcraft laws. (The last went to the gallows at Exeter in 1684.) The importance of the Chelmsford trial derives from the eminence of those taking part. No less a person than the Attorney General was employed in the prosecution. Precedent plays a

52

major part in English justice, and this trial set a pattern which was to be copied in later ones, particularly in the way rules of evidence were set aside. It was followed by the publication of a sensational 'chapbook', one of the series which includes our own source-book—Potts' *Discovery of Witches in the County of Lancaster*. These chapbooks, popularly written accounts of dramatic trials, were still being hawked in the streets of London in the last century. No pact with the Devil and no witches' sabbat were mentioned, but the other common features of later trials were there. Most of the harm spoken of by witnesses could be put down to trivial domestic accidents or ordinary illness. Unsupported and ridiculous confessions were believed; evidence of children was accepted and familiars, in the shape of white cats or black dogs, sucked blood from the witches in exchange for their generous but largely unkept promises of power and worldly wealth. In a later trial at Chelmsford, in 1582, seven- and eight-year-old children were giving evidence, and there were familiars everywhere.

On 24 March 1603, Queen Elizabeth of England died, acknowledging on her deathbed that James, 'our cousin from Scotland', was her heir. He left Edinburgh on 5 April that year and made a slow but popular and triumphal progress to London, conferring numerous knighthoods on the way south. Hard years were ahead for those accused as witches. In the proclamation of general pardon which marked his accession 'wytchcrafte' was specifically and ominously excluded from the amnesty. A new edition of *Demonology* appeared in 1603, then in 1604 came the strictest of any English laws aimed at witches.

In the decade which followed the passing of this Act the percentage of accused witches eventually put to death rose higher than ever before, although even in this period less than half the accused ended on the gallows. With this law we reach the final definition, so far as England was concerned, of what a witch was supposed to be: a woman, or man, who had abandoned Christianity and renounced her baptism, who wor-

53

shipped Satan as her God and had made a definite act of surrendering herself to him, body and soul, offering herself as an instrument for the evil work he could only perform through a human agent. In exchange she had been promised anything she desired to have. She was provided with a familiar spirit which was to be allowed to suck her blood, and the Devil's mark was put on her. The new law kept much of the phraseology of Elizabeth's Act, which it repealed. But hanging was now prescribed for those found guilty not only of murder, but of invocation of spirits, theft of corpses or causing bodily injury. Death was prescribed for second convictions under other headings: divination of treasure, recovery of lost property, procuring of unlawful love or proved intent to do bodily harm.

> Be it enacted . . . that if any person or persons . . . shall use, practise, or exercise any invocation, or conjuration, of any evil and wicked spirit, or shall consult, covenant with, entertain, employ, feed, or reward any evil or wicked spirit to or for any intent or purpose, or . . . take up any dead man, woman, or child out of his, her, or their grave, or any other place where the dead body resteth, or the skin, bone, or any other part of any dead person, to be employed or used in any manner of witchcraft, sorcery, charm, or enchantment: or . . . shall use, practise, or exercise any witchcraft, enchantment, charm, or sorcery, whereby any person shall be killed, destroyed, wasted, consumed, pined or lamed in his or her body, or any part thereof . . . every such offender or offenders, their aides, abettors and counsellors, being of any of the said offences duly and lawfully convicted . . . shall suffer pains of death as a felon or felons, and shall lose the privilege and benefit of clergy and sanctuary.

Some of these terms need explanation. In law all crimes more serious than petty offences were either treason, felonies or misdemeanors. Treason is a crime against someone to whom the accused has a bond of loyalty. A subject plotting the death of the king, or assaulting his person, is guilty of high treason, a woman compassing the death of her husband is guilty of petty treason. This class of crime, unlike witchcraft, was punishable by burning, and as late as 1726, years after the last witch had

54

died on the gallows, a woman was burnt at the stake in England for killing her husband. A felon, originally, was a criminal, part of whose punishment had been to forfeit land or goods to the Crown, whereas no such forfeiture was exacted in the case of the less serious class of crime—misdemeanor. Examples of felony were murder, rape, robbery and arson. Perjury or attempting without success to commit a felony were misdemeanors. The ancient legal distinction between the two classes of crime was abolished by the Criminal Justices Act of 1967. The dividing line had become blurred and the differences often ridiculous. It was pointed out, when the new Bill was being debated, that whilst to steal a penny was a felony, the fraudulent conversion of many thousands of pounds was technically a misdemeanor.

Privilege, or benefit, of clergy is commonly misunderstood, the expression 'without benefit of clergy' being often wrongly taken to mean the disposal of the body of a hanged criminal without a Christian burial. It was not this at all. Privilege originated from the pious regard in which the early Church was held, and it exempted the clergy, in some cases, from the normal criminal proceedings taken before a secular judge. It was later extended to include those who were sufficiently well educated to be able to read, so that it became necessary to state specifically, in laws like the Witchcraft Acts, that Benefit of Clergy could not be claimed. The privilege was abolished in 1827 for all except peers, who retained it until 1841. At one time a person who 'claimed his clergy' was branded before release. A branding-iron, once used for this purpose, is still kept and shown to visitors in the Court Room at Lancaster. The brand bears a letter 'M' for malefactor, and was used on the thumb.

From this same superstitious attitude towards the Church came the institution of sanctuary. Except for treason or sacrilege, a criminal could find sanctuary against the law by taking refuge in a church or churchyard or in some specified privileged place in our big cities. He was then usually given a safe conduct to a prescribed port and banished from the country, instead of suffering the normal punishment for his crime. As this privilege was not abolished until 1623, it was necessary in drafting the Witchcraft Acts to state clearly that escape through this loophole, like claiming benefit of clergy, would not be tolerated.

The practice of judges touring the country on recognised circuits was started by Henry II. It was then a means by which local administration of a thoroughly rustic country could be in some measure controlled by the central government. Each Assize town was visited three or four times a year. The practice still goes on today although it is under review. In 1612 all cases for the county of Lancashire were heard at Lancaster where Potts described how:

> The Circuite of the North partes being now almost ended. The 16. of August.
> Vpon Sunday in the after noone, my honourable Lords and Iudges of Assize, came from Kendall to Lancaster.

The judges were Sir James Altham and Sir Edward Bromley:

> Iustices of Assize, Oyer and Terminor, and generall Gaole deliuerie in the circuit of the North Parts.

The expression 'Oyer and Terminor' means simply 'to hear and to determine'. In other words the judges had a commission from Parliament to hear and judge the cases against prisoners awaiting them in the gaols.

On the arrival of the judges 'M. Couell, presented vnto their Lordships a Calender, conteyning the Names of the Prisoners committed to his charge.' A list of prisoners or suspects awaiting trial is still called a calendar, and anyone interested in some lurid old cases is recommended to the selection published under the title of the *Newgate Calendar*.

Although by modern standards hasty, the trials about to start were not irregular. In the case of the Pendle group of witches a complaint had been made to a justice of the peace, who had enquired into it and found sufficient evidence to commit the accused to the Assizes. The trials were in open court, not secret, and following the usual practice each prisoner was arraigned, ie called to the bar of the court, where the indictment was read out to her. She was then asked to plead 'Guilty' or 'Not Guilty'. All but one pleaded 'Not Guilty' whereupon a jury was sworn and the trial proceeded. There was no question of verdicts being decided beforehand. The various juries having heard the confessions and evidence presumably tried to reach unbiased judgments, bearing in mind the ideas current in those times, ideas which the jurymen would share. As in other English trials some of the accused were acquitted and the case against the Samlesbury Witches, as we shall hear, collapsed.

But, just as in times of war and national emergency liberal laws are altered and suspended, so, in dealing with people in league with supernatural powers of evil, special measures had to be taken. No prisoner was given a chance to prepare a defence. She may not even have known, before the trial, the actual charges against her. One of the chief witnesses was a girl of nine. Hearsay evidence was accepted and the confessions of accomplices were regarded as particularly cogent. King James had written: 'Who but witches can be proofs, and so witnesses to the doings of witches?' Judges renowned for their wisdom and fairness in other fields sometimes allowed evidence which would have been rejected in any but a witch trial, and passed severe or capital sentences on the strength of it. At the time of the trials of Lancashire Witches, the judges had a powerful reason for seeking the conviction of suspects—the known opinions and writings of their king, who had it in his power to dismiss them.

As would be the practice today the two judges divided the cases between them and on Tuesday afternoon, 18 August, Judge Bromley, coming into the hall, announced that he now intended to proceed with the trial of witches. He ordered that all Justices of the Peace who had examined prisoners, and all who were to give evidence against them, should attend. The Sheriff was then commanded to present his prisoners and prepare a jury of gentlemen 'for Life and Death'.

The Trial of Chattox

The first to face this jury was Anne Whittle, alias Chattox, 'Widdow, about the age of Fourescore yeares, or there-aboutes'. After her eighty years of poverty there is no reason to dispute Potts' description of her: '. . . a very old withered spent and decreped creature, her sight almost gone. . . . Her lippes euer chattering and walking [meaning working or talking] but no man knew what.' Her nickname is unexplained. Crossley's suggestion that it derived from her palsied chattering is a feasible one, or it could have been a corruption of Chadwick or Chadwicks, perhaps her maiden name, and very common in the Pendle area.

Potts concedes that although she was a dangerous witch she nevertheless dealt plainly and truly in court, and but for the enormity of her crimes her contrition would have moved them to pity.

She was charged with having killed, eighteen or nineteen years previously, by the force of her witchcraft, Robert Nutter of Greenhead. She was not charged with the deaths of Alizon's father, John Device, little Anne Nutter, Hugh Moore and the infant John Moore of Higham, for all of which, Alizon Device had told Nowell, she was responsible. She pleaded 'Not Guilty' whereupon Nowell asked that her statement to him written down at Fence on 2 April should be read. This, with its admission to being a witch and its revealing explanation of young Robert Nutter's lack of warmth towards her family—her daughter in particular—was followed by the reading of Demdike's statement of the same date, in which she had told of seeing Chattox and Anne Redfearn with three pictures of clay.

It is often impossible to decide what evidence given in Potts' book is that read from statements, what was given verbally in court, and what he copied from documents available to him. After printing one further statement—James Robinson's—he points out that there is already sufficient to convict Chattox

58

'since the voluntarie confession of a Witch doth exceede all other euidence'. So the testimonies of James and Alizon Device, none of which had any bearing on the death of Robert Nutter, were probably not used at Lancaster although, as he had them before him, he copied them in.

Whatever fear Chattox might once have inspired, or whatever powers she might once have had, she was powerless, as King James had promised all witches should be, when prosecuted by the law. At the end of her short trial she tearfully acknowledged all the evidence to be true, asked God for mercy and forgiveness, and prayed for his mercy on her daughter Anne Redfearn, waiting to be tried. She pathetically said that her familiar Fancie, who fourteen years before had promised gold, silver and worldly wealth, had not only deserted her but had taken away most of her sight. She had last seen him in the likeness of a bear, gaping as though he would have worried her. When she would not speak to him he pulled her down to the ground!

Elizabeth Device

Old Chattox was not convicted, or sentenced immediately. Her trial was straightway followed by that of Demdike's daughter Elizabeth, 'late wife of John Device', who when he died believed it was because of his default in paying protection money. Her mother was eighty, her own youngest child was nine, so she was probably in her late forties. She was a very ugly woman, having, says Potts 'a preposterous marke in Nature . . . her left eye standing lower than the other, the one looking downe, the other looking vp . . . so strangely deformed as the best that were present in that great Audience did affirme they had not often seene the like.' Her case must have caused much more stir and excitement than Chattox's just concluded. There was not much contrition here; instead she made such a scene that she had to be taken from the courtroom before the trial could proceed.

She was charged with three murders by witchcraft: those of

59

John Robinson of Barley, his brother James and, in collusion with her mother and Alice Nutter, Henry Mitton of Roughlee. She had already confessed to all these at the enquiry conducted by Nowell and Bannister on 27 April, when Jennet and James had been persuaded by the magistrates to denounce their mother before she was confronted. And it begins to look as though, in the three months that elapsed between the arrests and the trial, Nowell had coached little Jennet, the only one of her family left free, until she was word-perfect enough to be produced as his star witness in the courtroom. Potts was suitably wonderstruck that it had 'pleased God to raise vp a yong maid, her owne daughter, to discouer all their Practices, Meetings, Consultations, Murthers, Charmes and Villainies'. But when Elizabeth saw Jennet in court she cursed outrageously, and cried out against her so that the child was soon in tears and had to tell the judge that she could not continue. He could not quieten Elizabeth, or stop her denying her own confession, so he ordered that she be led away. Jennet was then set on a table so that all might see and hear her better.

Her evidence consisted of a statement to the effect that she knew her mother to be a witch of three or four years' standing. She had several times seen her spirit, the brown dog called Ball, come to their house at Malkin Tower and speak with her; and Ball, instructed by her mother, had been instrumental in killing both John and James Robinson, and Henry Mitton. This evidence was followed by the reading of part of James Device's confession, taken before Nowell and Bannister, designed to show that Elizabeth had been the chief instigator of the now notorious meeting when she had played hostess to the assembled witches. At some stage Elizabeth must have been brought back into court and while she once again impudently denied the accusations and her own confession and cried out against her children, she at last lost hope and with the law and her own family ranged against her gave in and begged the court for mercy.

James Device

This lad, when brought to the bar, was 'so insensible, weake and vnable in all thinges, that he could neither speake, heare, or stand'. He had to be held up, and Potts concedes that his pitiable condition might have been occasioned by his long sojourn in the cell. Gaolers had complete power over their charges and the treatment they received usually depended on the money they could pay. The poor were herded together regardless of age, sex or crime. This state of affairs lasted into the nineteenth century, as any reader of Dickens will know. George Fox, founder of the Quakers, one of whose visionary experiences took place on the summit of Pendle, was imprisoned at Lancaster in 1644. He has left us a harrowing account of prison life and although he was not chained in a dungeon like a suspected witch he had to endure a cold winter in prison and, like James Device fifty years before him, he became so weak that on release he could not stand without support.

Weak-minded or not, James Device was nevertheless charged with the murders by witchcraft of Anne, wife of Henry Towneley of Carr Hall and John Duckworth, of the Laund. Roger Nowell asked that Anne Towneley's husband might be called—he was present in court and prepared to give evidence—but Potts maddeningly excuses himself from reporting what Master Towneley said, maintaining that there was sufficient matter in the written evidence to prove James' guilt. This is true, but any statement by someone of reasonable intelligence and standing would have been welcome leaven amongst the lumps of nonsense, nowhere worse than in James' confession, which Potts was willing to copy.

James, on 27 April, had admitted to both the murders with which he was now charged, and when his statement was read out to him he acknowledged it to be true. Nevertheless, Jennet was again produced and she confirmed the details of the killing of Anne Towneley. She was indeed busily helping to condemn her family to the gallows and 'although she were very yong yet it was wonderfull to the Court in so great a Presence and Audience, with what modestie, gouernment and vnderstanding shee deliuered this Euidence against the Prisoner at the Barre, being her owne naturall brother'.

The court had not yet finished with James and he was now indicted for the deaths of John Hargreaves of Goldshaw Booth and Blaze Hargreaves of Higham. He pleaded not guilty to these charges, crimes to which he had so far not confessed, but his sister Jennet was again called. She said very briefly that James, whom she knew to have been a witch for three years, had killed John and Blaze Hargreaves. No motives were mentioned but she said that Dandie, his familiar, had helped in both murders, each time appearing at Malkin Tower in the shape of a black dog and being told by his master to take the lives of the two men. At the end of James' trial Judge Bromley had the various written depositions shown to the jury before they were called upon to consider their verdicts. They found Anne Whittle, alias Chattox, Elizabeth Device and James Device guilty of all the indictments against them, thus successfully disposing of three murder trials in the space of a few hours.

Anne Redfearn

For anyone reading through Potts that would appear to have been the end of Tuesday's proceedings, for he devotes twenty-four pages to the trial of the Samlesbury Witches which took place the following day. But, when he returns again to the Pendle Witches, we read that Anne Redfearn, Chattox's daughter, had been tried on the Tuesday night for her part in bringing about the death of Robert Nutter and others not specified. She was acquitted on these charges, so Potts gives no account of this trial beyond saying that the evidence against her 'was not very pregnant'. Anne was the only one of the original four women sent to prison at the beginning of April who never confessed to witchcraft. Except for her plea of 'Not Guilty' no single word of hers is recorded. Having been acquitted on Tuesday of the death of her would-be seducer, Anne was now charged on the Wednesday with the murder of his father, Christopher Nutter, who, eighteen or nineteen years before, had scorned his son's request to have the family turned off their land and put in gaol.

Exactly the same statements that were used against her mother were read in court as evidence against Anne: Demdike's tale of the three clay 'pictures', John Nutter's story of the conversation between his brother and father on a walk home from Burnley, and Margaret Crook's brief account of the deaths, within a few months of each other, of first her brother and then her father. In fact the only real charge connecting the accused with her victim was Old Demdike's statement, which was read out, that one of the three pictures she had seen was of Christopher Nutter. James Device had also told of seeing the three Redfearns, Thomas, Anne, and their daughter Marie, each holding a clay model, but he said he did not know whose images they were.

Following his usual habit, Thomas Potts, having filled three pages with statements already familiar to us, continues: 'Likewise many witnesses [were] examined vpon oth, viua voce, who charged her with many strange practices and declared the death of the parties.' Her mother, already condemned, and probably with no illusions about the inevitable sentence, was brought back into court and seems to have again tried to save Anne's life. At the end of her own trial she had prayed the judge to be merciful to her daughter, and she now confessed to making the clay pictures herself and entreated the court, on her knees, to spare Anne. We can feel much sympathy for Anne Redfearn, who left a husband and at least one child, and admire the apparent strength of character which enabled her to resist the magistrates and remain unrepentant to the end.

Alice Nutter

In his introduction to the trial of Alice Nutter, when trying to account for her involvement with witchcraft, Potts makes it absolutely clear that he possessed, or had access to, a copy of King James' book *Demonology*. Mistress Nutter belonged to a better class of society than the destitute peasants with whom she now found herself. 'It is certaine,' writes Potts, 'she was a rich woman, had a great estate and children of good hope.' He then explains: 'The two degrees of persons which chiefly practise Witchcraft, are such, as are in great miserie and pouertie, for such the Deuill allures to follow him, by promising great riches. . . . Others, though rich, yet burne in a desperate desire of Reuenge; Hee allures them by promises, to get their turne satisfied to their hearts contentment.' This last paragraph is a word-for-word quotation from James I's book, and to be so exact must have been copied from it.

There are other reasons besides her status why the name of Richard Nutter's wife is so well remembered locally. Her house, Roughlee Hall, is still standing, and indeed occupied. Nutter is still a common name in the district and nearly all who bear it keep her name alive by claiming her as an ancestor; but perhaps the principal reason for her fame is that both Harrison Ainsworth and Robert Neill gave this mysterious woman, about whom we really know so little, a major part in their novels.

Roughlee Hall, the home of Alice Nutter, and the most tangible connection we have with the Lancashire Witches

At her trial she was charged with the murder (in concert with Old Demdike and Elizabeth Device), of Henry Mitton of Roughlee, and was convicted on the statements of James and Elizabeth and the evidence of little Jennet, all of whom said she had been at the fateful meeting at Malkin Tower. James added that he had heard his grandmother talk of killing Mitton by witchcraft, helped by his mother and Alice Nutter, the old woman giving as her reason that Mitton had once refused her request for a penny. The charge of the murder of Mitton was as reasonable as any of the charges brought against the other women, but the reason for the supposed murder, that he had been killed for refusing to give Demdike a penny, was ludicrous when considered against this particular prisoner, even bearing in mind the value of a penny in those days, when a labourer's daily wage was twopence 'with meat', or sixpence without.

The depositions of the three Devices were read in court; then, in Potts' record, follows the description of an identity parade arranged by the judge to test Jennet. This is the only incident in the trial which comes anywhere near to a questioning of evidence. We can regard it, as Potts did, as another manifestation of the extreme care taken by Judge Bromley with this particular woman, or we can dismiss it as a device to add a little conviction to fairly flimsy evidence of evil-doing. Or perhaps, after the revelations of the Samlesbury trial, when the evidence of a girl not much older than Jennet had been shown to be pure invention, the judge was in a cautious frame of mind. He had Jennet taken to the Upper Hall, then commanded the gaoler, Covell, to line up the supposed witches, mixed with other prisoners, and some strange women not directly concerned with the case. Jennet was then brought back and closely examined by Bromley as to the names of the women who were at Malkin Tower on Good Friday. She was asked if she would know their faces if she saw them and declared that she would, 'whereupon she went and tooke Alice Nutter . . . by the hand, and accused her

to be one: and told her in what place shee sat . . . and who sat
next her'.

Still Bromley had not finished. Did Jennet know Joan a
Style he asked? (Joan a Style was one of the arbitrary names
used by lawyers in discussing legal cases before the briefer
modern substitutes Mr A, Madam X, etc came into use.) But
'No,' replied Jennet, she knew no such woman, in fact had
never heard the name! It is a noticeable feature of the examinations and trials that only the poorer and simpler of the
accused were persuaded to confess: the two old women, Elizabeth, although she denied it later, James, and Alizon.

Alice Nutter confessed nothing. Why family influence and
connections could not save her is a mystery. She was impenitent
to the end, leaving us with the difficult task of explaining her
connection, if any, with witchcraft, a connection which also
puzzled Thomas Potts. Following his mention of her riches and
estate he had gone on to describe her as 'of good temper, free
from enuy or malice; yet whether by the meanes of the rest of
the Witches, or some vnfortunate occasion shee was drawne to
fall to this wicked course of life, I know not.'

Katherine Hewitt

Next to face the court was Katherine Hewitt, one of the two
women from Colne present at Malkin Tower (the other being
Alice Gray). The wife of John Hewitt, her husband's occupa-
tion is given as clothier—a term which did not then have the
same meaning in all parts of England. In the North it could
mean a weaver, in other parts it could signify the man who
supplied the yarn, paid for its manufacture and arranged its
sale. But at least we can surmise that she was a little above the
peasant level of the Demdikes and Chattoxes. She was also
known by the nickname 'Mouldheels'.

Katherine was charged with the murder of a Colne child,
Anne Foulds. The relevant part of James' statement on 27 April
was read out. He had said that she was at Malkin Tower and

66

that she, along with Alice Gray, had confessed to having killed 'Fould's wife's child' and to having 'in hancke' a child of Michael Hartley's of Colne. The origin of the term 'in hancke' is uncertain. Crossley, in a note in the Chetham Society's edition of the *Discovery*, suggests it might be an abbreviation of 'to handkill', ie murder, or that it might derive from the Scots verb 'to hanck' meaning 'to hold'. On a later page of Potts 'hancke' is indeed replaced by 'gotten holde of', but whatever its derivation its meaning is unmistakable: Hartley's child was in the process of being bewitched to death.

Part of Elizabeth's statement was next read; it supported James'. Then, as Potts reports it, there followed a repetition of the identity parade first used in the case of Alice Nutter. There is another such in the next trial and although they read as having been separate, it is hardly likely that Covell would have been asked to waste the court's time in linking up witches, ordinary prisoners and other strange women three times, and Jennet's picking out of the women she recognised could have been done at one occasion. However this charade was conducted, Jennet took Katherine by the hand, accused her of being at Malkin Tower, described where she sat and who sat next to her, and what talk they had between them. As a cunning variation Bromley this time enquired of Jennet if 'Joan a Downe' (Madam Y?) was at the feast, but she replied again that she knew no such woman, and in fact had never heard the name. Katherine Hewitt had pleaded 'Not Guilty' like all the others before her. No confession is recorded, nor any other evidence. The jury then delivered their verdicts, finding the Samlesbury Witches not guilty, but declaring that Anne Redfearn, Alice Nutter and Katherine Hewitt were all guilty of the felonies and murders contained in the indictments against them. Master Covell then brought forth for trial John Bulcock, Jane Bulcock his mother, and Alizon Device.

John and Jane Bulcock

Jane, wife of Chris Bulcock, and her son John, lived at Moss
End. This house, near Newchurch, is next to Bull Hole, whose
tenant had asked Demdike to cure his sick cow. The Bulcocks
were accused of having feloniously practised their devilish and
wicked art upon the body of Jennet Deane of Newfield Edge,
so that by force of witchcraft, she wasted and consumed and
eventually went mad.

*Moss End Farm, now derelict. On this site in 1612 stood the house of John
Bulcock and his mother Jane*

Again Potts reports an identity parade and although, like
Katherine Hewitt, the Bulcocks were not amongst the half-
dozen witches Jennet had been able to name, she took Jane
Bulcock by the hand and said she had been at Malkin Tower,
and when she came to John she added the interesting detail

68

that he had turned the spit on which the meat had roasted for their meal.

Next a part of James' confession was read out, a part in which he seems to have been even more incoherent than usual. Witness this: 'the said Iohn Bulcock, and Iane his said Mother, did confesse vpon Good-Friday last at the said Malking Tower, in the hearing of this Examinate, That they had bewitched, at the newfield Edge in Yorkshire, a woman called Iennet, wife of Iohn Deyne, besides her reason; and the said Woman's name so bewitched he did not heare them speake of!'

What are we to make of that? And as though James' ramblings are not enough, in reporting this trial Potts is at his most maddening. He says that when brought up for trial the Bulcocks impudently swore they were never at Malkin Tower 'at the Barre hauing formerly confessed'! Then he leaves us in some doubt about their fate. The crime of which they were accused, although not murder, carried the death penalty. The jury acquitted them. Yet they are included in the list of condemned prisoners sentenced to death by the judge, and in his introduction to their trial Potts tells us that they cried out in a very violent manner 'euen to the gallows, where they died impenitent for anything we know, because they died silent'!

Alizon Device

Perhaps because, like the Bulcocks who went before her and the woman who followed, she was not accused of murder, the girl who was the first to be examined by Nowell was the last of his prisoners to be tried. Alizon Device, daughter of Elizabeth, sister of Jennet and James and granddaughter of Old Demdike, was probably in her late teens, whether older or younger than her brother we cannot be sure. In recent years she had been her grandmother's support when they went a-begging.

Her victim, John Law the pedlar, despite his condition, had attended all the Assizes and was waiting by the Moot Hall in the Castle to be called. Potts describes him: 'his head drawne awrie, his Eyes and face deformed, His speech not well to bee vnderstood, his Thighes and Legges starcke lame: his Bodie able to indure no trauell.' In this distressful state he was led into court by his son and Alizon was charged with having been the cause of his deformities. On seeing him, having not yet pleaded 'Guilty' or 'Not Guilty' she straightway fell on her knees and tearfully pleaded to be heard. So Judge Bromley had her separated from the other prisoners and required her to make an open declaration of her offence. This, says Potts, agreed verbatim with her confession of 30 March.

The crowd in court now heard, from Alizon's own lips, of her initiation, at Demdike's prompting, into witchcraft, and of the events in Colne on 19 March which had led to the start of the witch-hunt; and this liberal and voluntary confession, justifying as it did all Nowell's actions and confirming so much of what the king had written, particularly about the method of entry into the craft, amazed everyone. To confirm the story Law was ordered by the judge to tell, on oath, how he had been handled on this unlucky day. His story differed little from Alizon's: he told of his encounter with the girl, of his stroke, and of being carried into the ale-house. He told how, as he lay there in great pain, not able to stir either hand or foot, he saw a great black dog standing by him with fearful fiery eyes, great teeth and a terrible countenance, looking him in the face. Whereat he was very sore afraid: and immediately after came in Alizon Device, who stood not long there but looked on him and went away. After which time he was tormented both day and night with the said Alizon Device: and so continued lame, not able to travel or take pains ever since that time.

By now Law was crying and turning to the prisoner he declared with passion, 'This thou knowest to be true!' Alizon made no denials, only asking that God and the pedlar might forgive her wicked offence. Hereabouts Roger Nowell stood up and asked that the statement made at Read on 30 March by Abraham Law, when he had searched out Alizon and brought her to him, might be read. Only on the small matter of the pins did it disagree with what the court had already heard. Alizon had said that she wanted to buy them, the pedlar maintained that she wanted them given, Abraham had it that she offered to buy some pins, had then been found to have no money to pay for them, but was given them anyway.

Thus ended the evidence against Alizon. Considerable solicitude was shown for the pedlar who had evidently been a stout man of goodly stature—a type very susceptible to strokes! Alizon was asked if she could not restore him to his former health but she, and the rest of the witches, said they could not, adding to little purpose that had Old Demdike lived she could and would have helped him out of his misery. Several gentlemen present expressed their concern at his condition and when he was discharged the judge promised that something would be done for his relief and maintenance. The jury then returned verdicts of 'Not Guilty' for John and Jane Bulcock, and for Alizon, convicted on her own confession, 'Guilty'.

Margaret Pearson

That was the end of the cases prepared by Roger Nowell. The next one was the concern of Nicholas Bannister, Nowell's neighbour, from Altham, who had sat with him during his enquiries at Fence. The accused, Margaret Pearson, was the wife of Edward Pearson of Padiham, a market town then the equal of Burnley, but now vastly outgrown by its faster developing neighbour. Of her trial at least three features are of interest: the fact that it was her third, the sentence she received, and the description of her familiar. We know of her other trials that the first was for murder and the second for bewitching a neighbour. This time she was charged with harming a fellow citizen's goods in that she had, by her devilish and wicked arts, killed a mare, the property of one Dodgson, of Padiham.

Margaret was evidently known to the Pendle Witches, although this acquaintance was perhaps only from having shared

71

the same cell, and Old Chattox, already tried and sentenced, was hauled back to speak against her. The accused, said Chattox, was a very evil woman, as evil as herself in fact, and had a spirit which had first appeared to her in the likeness of a cloven-footed man. This is the only mention in Potts of a figure familiar from many old witch-drawings. Chattox went on to say that the accused had confessed to her the murder of one Childer's wife and daughter, and had told her how Dodgson's horse was done to death. Margaret and her spirit had climbed into the stable through a loop-hole and sat on the wretched mare until it collapsed and died!

Altham is adjacent to Padiham, and it looks as though Nicholas Bannister had been conducting his own examination into the case of Margaret Pearson, who lived almost on his doorstep. Potts tells us how the depositions and examinations concerning the death of the mare were many, but selects just one—Jennet Booth's, given on 9 August, only a week before the trial opened. Bannister had examined Jennet on his own and evidently considered her silly testimony worth recording and presenting to the court. It amounted to this: a few days after Pearson's wife had been committed to Lancaster, Jennet Booth had gone to his house to card wool. There she was given a pan of milk for her child and she boiled this on a rather poor fire. When it was taken off there was a toad, 'or a thing very like a toad', which to her thinking had come out of the fire. It was lifted in a pair of tongs and carried from the house. Weighty evidence indeed to persuade a jury to find Margaret guilty! But they did. It must be that at her first two trials she had been acquitted, otherwise, even though not guilty of murder, she would have been sentenced to death. Instead she was condemned to 'stand vpon the Pillarie in open Market, at Clitheroe, Padiham, Whalley and Lancaster, foure Market dayes, with a Paper vpon your head, in great Letters, declaring your offence, and there you shall confesse your offence, and after to remain in Prison for one yeare without Baile. . . .'

The wording of the Act makes it clear that the offender was to be exposed, for a period of six hours, once in every quarter, on a market or fair day, and was openly to confess her offence. The towns chosen for her public humiliations involved her making long journeys from Lancaster, the nearest of the other three places being a good twenty miles from the gaol. It emphasises the point that this pillorying, besides being a punishment for the convicted, was meant to draw publicity to the fact that crime, even in those days, did not pay. The pillory was then a familiar sight in every market town—a cross of wood behind which the victim stood, secured by the neck and perhaps also

Margaret Pearson was sentenced to stand in the pillory in the open market
(*taken from an old woodcut*)

the wrists. The degree of humiliation suffered would depend on the public's reaction: they were not always prepared to plaster the victim with bad eggs and rotting vegetables. On the other hand many died in the pillory, killed by stones thrown by the mob. Margaret Pearson does not appear to have been at Malkin Tower, although Grace Hay, another woman from Padiham, was. We hear no more of Grace. Perhaps she was another who fled the district and successfully escaped.

Last to be tried was the complete outsider, Isobel Roby. Potts reports her trial, as a result of which she was found guilty, but as she had no connection with Pendle, Padiham or Samlesbury an account of its one or two interesting features is held over to the next chapter.

Thus was concluded the trial of witches, nineteen in two days. After three solemn orders for silence Thomas Potts presented the list of prisoners to the judge. Brought back to the bar of the court to hear their fate were Old Chattox and her daughter Anne, Elizabeth Device and her two children, James and Alizon, Alice Nutter and Katherine Hewitt, Jane Bulcock and her son John (although the only recorded verdict in their case had been 'Not Guilty'), and Isobel Roby.

In his address to the prisoners awaiting sentence the judge asked them to consider their good fortune in having been granted so careful a trial, and to thank God that he had seen fit to disclose their wickedness before their souls were irretrievably damned. He recommended those who had not done so to confess and ask forgiveness of those they had wronged, and then said: 'You shall all goe from hence, to the Castle from whence you came, from thence you shall bee carried to the place of Execution for this Countie, where your bodies shall bee hanged vntill you be dead. And GOD HAVE MERCIE VPON YOVR SOVLES.' He appointed a learned and worthy preacher, probably William Leigh of Standish, to help them to prepare for the next world.

Those found not guilty were called to be addressed by the

74

judge. These were Elizabeth Astley, John Ramsden, Alice Gray, Isabel Sidegraves and Lawrence Hay. Potts did not record any of their trials and we do not know for sure where four of these people came from. They were all listed as Samlesbury Witches, but this is a mistake, at least in the case of Alice Gray who came from Colne and had been present at Malkin Tower. It may be wrong for the others. From the statements of James and Elizabeth Device, Alice Gray appears to have been a companion of Katherine Hewitt's. She confessed, they said, to the murder of the child Anne Foulds, and to having the intention of killing Michael Hartley's child. So here is another mystery. Her crimes were the same as Katherine Hewitt's, they were both at Malkin Tower, yet one was hanged and the other acquitted. No identity parade is mentioned, no trial recorded.

The judge warned these five not to presume on their good fortune, as he had no doubt there were those amongst them who were as guilty as some of those sentenced. They had to promise to be of good behaviour and to appear at the next Assizes.

Potts gives no account of the executions. He may not even have seen them. All he says is that they were carried out 'the next day following' the sentence, and we do not need to be particularly bloodthirsty or morbid to agree with Crossley who wrote, in a footnote to the Chetham edition: 'We could have dispensed with many of the flowers of rhetoric with which the pages of this discovery are strewn, if Master Potts would have favoured us with a plain, unvarnished account of what occurred at this execution.' Whatever occurred there is no doubt that the multitudes attracted to Lancaster by the trials would regard the gruesome performance as the climax of their outing. Public hangings were specifically designed to impress, and awe, the populace. People were encouraged to watch them, and to this end public announcements of impending executions were made. It was considered that the macabre spectacles would act as deterrents to would-be law-breakers. Hangings were multiple affairs; old drawings often show five or six hanging from the

75

same beam, and a contemporary account of executions at Lancaster says 'the gallows were in frequent use, as many as ten being hanged at one time'. The gallows, consisting basically of a cross-beam of stout wood, supported at both ends, could be either permanent or temporary. Sometimes there were two beams, even three (at Tyburn for instance where this most famous 'gallows tree' was triangular—its site now marked by a brass plate in the road, very near Marble Arch). Condemned prisoners mounted a ladder, or stood on a platform or in a cart; then a noose was put round their necks. They jumped, or were pushed from their support, or the cart was driven away from under them. Whatever the method, death was more often than not by strangulation, and the suffering, and the culprits' desperate struggles for breath, were often prolonged.

Thus, about a mile from the dungeon where they had spent the months of summer, ended the lives of the Lancashire Witches. The judges and their clerk could move on, the magistrates and those who had attended to give evidence could return to their homes and sleep more soundly in their beds, Covell could resume charge of his partially emptied gaol.

We do not know who took charge of little Jennet, but twenty-one years later the little girl whom God had raised up in 1612 to be one of the instruments of his justice again came to Lancaster. By then she herself was a God-forsaken witch.

CHAPTER IV

More Witch Trials

THE three trials with which this chapter is concerned bear, in different ways, on those just concluded. Jennet Preston was at Malkin Tower, and only the fact of her living in Yorkshire assured for her a separate trial. It had many interesting features and illustrates particularly the liaison that existed between magistrates in neighbouring districts and, in this instance, counties.

The trial of the Samlesbury Witches displays the tragic ease with which, in the climate then prevailing, innocent women could find themselves in the dock listening to a convincing case being made out against them; and in Isobel Roby's trial we find mention of the probable source of much of the then current witch dogma, as well as a reference to 'wisemen'—the country healers often mistakenly called witches, a class to which some of the witches of Pendle might well have belonged.

Jennet Preston

It is ironical that while the men and women who gathered at Malkin Tower have become known to us as the Lancashire Witches, the first of this company to be hanged for her supposed crimes was a Yorkshire woman—Jennet Preston of Gisburn in Craven, a village only five miles from Pendle Hill, but just across the county border. She was tried at York on 27 July, and her judge was Bromley's colleague Sir James Altham. It was then a full fortnight before the two judges, on their circuit of

77

the North Parts, reached Lancaster by way of Kendal to try the rest of the witches. We have, however, followed the example of Thomas Potts. Although he wrote it first, he put the account of this isolated trial after the main ones from Lancaster.

The family supposed to have suffered at Jennet's hands were the Listers of Westby, which place is about half a mile from Gisburn, in the corner formed by the Clitheroe and Blacko roads. In his introduction to her trial Potts tells us that Jennet Preston was for long well thought of by the Listers, had free access to their house and was denied nothing of which she stood in need. This last statement suggests that she was a poor woman.

Thomas Lister died, at Bracewell, near Barnoldswick, in 1607, and was buried at Gisburn on 8 February. His son, also called Thomas, at first treated Jennet considerately as his father had done, but eventually his attitude changed. Losses in goods and cattle were blamed on her and her earlier trial at York at the Lent Assizes in 1612 for the murder of a child of 'one Dodgsonnes' was on Lister's instigation. The shadowy Dodgsons seem to have been great sufferers at the hands of witches. Margaret Pearson of Padiham we remember was said to have killed 'one Dodgson's mare'.

Jennet was acquitted in Lent, her judge this time being Bromley, who must have had his fill of witch trials that summer. She was released from York about 4 April, and seems to have made straight for home and Malkin Tower, for on Good Friday, within a week of her deliverance, she was consorting with the Pendle Witches at Elizabeth Device's home. She was again apprehended and taken back to York and the case against her was prepared by Thomas Heber of Marton, a magistrate whose daughter Jane the present Thomas Lister had married. Potts describes Heber as 'the best instructed of any man to present the evidence'—using a phrase which he repeated when explaining Nowell's prominent part in the Lancaster trial.

Jennet was indicted for killing by witchcraft the Thomas

78

Now the Ribblesdale Arms, this house was built by Thomas Lister whose grand-father Thomas, buried in the nearby churchyard, supposedly died of witchcraft, and whose father, also Thomas, had the satisfaction of seeing the witch Jennet Preston hanged

Lister who died in 1607—five years back! She pleaded 'Not Guilty', a jury was sworn and Heber then produced his witnesses and prayed that several examinations taken before Roger Nowell of Read and certified genuine, might be read in evidence against the accused. One Anne Robinson said that when Lister was in his last illness he cried out to the people around his bed: 'Iennet Preston [is] in the house, looke where shee is . . . for God's sake shut the doores and take her!'

Considered much more cogent was Anne's next statement, in which she was supported by Lister himself. Between them they deposed: 'that Iennet Preston, the Prisoner at the Barre, being brought to M. Lister, after hee was dead & layd out to be wound vp in his winding-sheet, the said Iennet Preston, coming

79

to touch the dead corpes, [it] bled fresh bloud presently, in the presence of all that were there present.'

We can trace this fanciful idea to *Demonology* where King James had written: 'In a secret murder, if the dead carcase be at any time thereafter handled by the murderer, it will gush out blood.'

It was not necessary for a person to have died of wounds for this manifestation to occur. Suspected murderers were sometimes made to touch the corpse, and the shoulder, hands and fingers are all mentioned as places from which blood flowed as the souls of the unwilling departed, unable to make sign or sound with their lifeless bodies, yet managing to agitate the still fluid blood and so denounce the killer. Fanciful or not, at the end of Jennet Preston's trial Altham drew the attention of the jury to this singular piece of evidence and more than anything else this persuaded them, after deliberating 'the most part of the day', to find her guilty.

Before the verdict and following the witnesses from Gisburn, James Device's account of the Good Friday meeting, as told to Nowell, was read out, with the emphasis on Jennet's part in it. According to James, who had, we remember, been taken over to Gisburn to identify her, she came to crave assistance from the rest of them for the killing of Master Lister. She told them how Lister had tried to have her put away at the last Assizes, and had then admitted that her power to harm was less than formerly, and for this reason she needed their help. They had all agreed, in James' hearing, to help her to dispose of Thomas Lister and another of the family, his brother Leonard 'when he came to live at the Sowgill'. This was a farm on the Pendle side of Gisburn.

James' evidence had ended with a reference to Jennet having had a spirit with her in the shape of a white foal. He had then confused this simple statement by his description of the dispersal of the witches in the afternoon. 'All the said Witches went out of the said house in their owne shapes and likenesses,

80

and they all, by that they were forth of the doores, were gotten on horsebacke like vnto Foales, some of one colour, some of another. And Preston's wife was the last. And when she got on horsebacke, they all presently vanished out of this Examinats sight.'

This begins to look like James' dim understanding of an idea put into his head by others, or else the rather careless invention of someone who was familiar with *Demonology*, for there the king had written: 'Some of them say that, for their journeys, they are transformed into the likeness of a little beast or foal.'

James' evidence concluded with the statement that they all agreed to meet at Jennet Preston's house 'this day twelvemonth', presumably Good Friday, 1613, and that should conference be needed in the meantime they should all meet upon 'Romles-Moore'. The nearest place with which this can be identified is Rombald's Moor, of which the more famous Ilkley Moor forms a part. It is at least fifteen miles from Gisburn. This statement by James is the only suggestion of any sort of regular meeting, and possibly contact, between witches from different parts. It might be taken to support the theories of those who would have us believe in a vast underground organisation of witches. But there are three things which dispute this. Firstly, when James was taken to Gisburn to identify Jennet, he needed to have 'full view of her' before he could be sure of her identity. This suggests that he had never met her before Good Friday although he had confessed to having been a witch for four years. Secondly, a meeting once every twelvemonth scarcely fits in with the idea of a monthly sabbat, and thirdly, Rombald's Moor, named after a legendary giant of that name, is so far distant from Pendle that it is more likely to be the invention of someone trying to show that distance was little object to witches than a serious suggestion as the venue for an emergency meeting.

Jennet was found guilty and hanged, confessing nothing and dying impenitent. Her husband, friends and kinsfolk were con-

F   81

vinced that she had been maliciously and wrongly persecuted by Thomas Lister and they went around for some time declaring this belief. However, we are told by Thomas Potts, they came to change their minds. Many of them made their way to the trial at Lancaster and her husband was in court when the judge was questioning Jennet Device and also when the girl was picking out, from the line of women assembled for her inspection, those at her mother's home at Easter. When Jennet said to the judge that she missed 'a woman that came out of Crauen', Old Preston, Potts tells us, 'cried out and went away, being fully satisfied his wife had Iustice and was worthie of death'.

The Samlesbury Witches

On the morning of Wednesday, 19 August, the Samlesbury Witches were tried at Lancaster. Chronologically their trial, which is fully reported, came between Anne Redfearn's first, when she was acquitted, and her second when she was found guilty. Potts lists the witches—the 'famous Salmesbury* Witches' as he calls them, thus:

> Jennet Bierley
> Ellen Bierley
> Jane Southworth
> John Ramsden
> Elizabeth Astley
> Alice Grey
> Isabell Sidegraves
> Lawrence Haye.

It has already been pointed out that Alice Gray is wrongly included and the only other reference, anywhere in the book, to John Ramsden, Elizabeth Astley, Isabell Sidegraves and Lawrence Haye is the brief information that they were acquitted, of what crimes we do not know, and bound over to be of good behaviour and to appear at the next Lancaster Assizes. And so

* The modern spelling, which we have used elsewhere, is Samlesbury.

the witches whose trials are recorded were Jennet Bierley, Ellen Bierley and Jane Southworth. The last of these, young and recently widowed, was a daughter of Richard Sherbourne of Stoneyhurst. The family into which she had married were manorial lords of Samlesbury for over three hundred years.

The most remarkable feature of the case was that although prepared by a magistrate, Robert Holden, whose standing was presumably similar to Nowell's, and depended as Nowell's had largely done on the evidence of a young girl related to one of the accused, the outcome was very different—the case collapsed and the three prisoners were freed. Potts justifies the verdict by analysing the evidence and displaying its shortcomings despite the fact that some of it was no more ridiculous than that presented in the other trials.

The principal witness was Grace, fourteen-year-old daughter of Thomas Sowerbutts, a husbandman. She was also the alleged victim. Jennet Bierley was her grandmother, Ellen Bierley her aunt, and they were indicted together with Jane Southworth, for bewitching Grace so that her body wasted and consumed. As in his dealings with Jennet Device the judge commanded the girl to point out the accused, and this she successfully did. She then said that she had seen her grandmother turn herself into a black dog which walked on two legs and spoke to her—in fact tried to persuade her to drown herself. The same dog, she said, had buried her in hay and straw in one Hugh Walshman's barn, then lain on top of her until she lost consciousness. Jennet and Ellen Bierley had taken her one night 'when the house was abed' to the home in Samlesbury of Thomas Walshman. There Jennet silently lifted a little child from bed, thrust a nail into its navel and sucked blood from the wound. She then returned the sleeping baby to the side of its parents. The child died some time later, whereupon, again taking Grace with them, the two women repaired at dead of night to Samlesbury churchyard and removed the little body from its grave. They carried it back to Jennet Bierley's house and made a meal of it, boiling some in a pot and broiling other parts on the coals. The bones were simmered and the women explained to the girl that with the fat they could make the ointment which would enable them to change into other shapes. Our witness said, as we would expect, that she refused to join in this cannibalism.

She went on to describe a meeting much closer to the sabbat of the witch books than the straightforward midday gathering at Malkin Tower. She told how she and the three women had been in the habit of going on Thursday and Sunday nights to a spot on the north side of the Ribble called Red Bank. There 'four black things, going upright, and yet not like men in the face' met them. After a meal of sorts they danced in pairs following which the women and Grace suffered their partners to pull them down and 'abuse their bodies'. That was the gist of the girl's statement. When asked by the judge to reply to these accusations the three women tearfully pleaded with him to examine Grace and enquire who had put her up to all this. At this challenge the girl's countenance fell, the other witnesses began to fall out amongst themselves and all Grace could counter to the judge's probings was that although she had been 'put to a master to learn' he had not prepared her for this.

It transpired that the master in question—a Roman Catholic priest calling himself Thompson—was really Christopher Southworth, of the same family as one of the accused. The background to the whole case was this: attempts to suppress Roman Catholicism had been less successful in Lancashire than anywhere else in the kingdom. As Potts complained: 'this Countie of Lancaster hath good store [of priests], who, by reason of the generall entertainement they find, and great maintenance they haue, resort hither, being farre from the Eye of Iustice.'

Families persisted in sending young men to Rome, or to the English colleges established in France, there to be trained as priests and then smuggled back into England to be hidden. These young men, if they were caught, faced a death more cruel

84

than that prescribed for witches. The Recusancy Laws (a re-
cusant was one who refused to attend Church of England services), made it high treason for a priest to say mass, and whereas
witches were hanged, the fate of those found guilty of high
treason was to be hanged, drawn and quartered. Many local
families bravely defied the Recusancy Laws and suffered in
consequence. The Towneleys of Burnley stoically endured the
very heavy fines imposed on them for refusing to give up their
faith. Towneley Hall was one of the many Lancashire houses with
its 'priest-hole', still shown to visitors today. John and Robert
Nutter of Pendle Forest were put to death as priests. Robert was
executed at Lancaster in 1600; John, after imprisonment in the
Marshalsea in Southwark, had been hanged, drawn and
quartered in 1584. We do not know their relationship to Alice
Nutter and their known beliefs cannot be taken to indicate that
she herself was a Roman Catholic.

When the judge's questions had forced Grace Sowerbutts to
admit that she was part of a fraudulent plot, the three accused
were removed from the court and William Leigh, the parson
and justice of the peace who came from Standish, was instructed
to take a statement from the girl. This is a complete admission
of invented evidence:

The Examination of Grace Sowerbvts of Salmesburie, taken
Wednesday, 19th. August 1612 . . . before William Leigh and
Edward Chisnal . . . by direction of Sir Edward Bromley, Knight
one of his Maiesties Iustices of Assize at Lancaster.
Being demanded whether the accusation shee laid vppon her
Grandmother Iennet Bierley, Ellen Bierley, and Iane Southworth of Witchcraft, viz. of the killing of the child of Thomas
Walshman, with a naile in the Nauell, the boyling, eating and
oyling, thereby to transforme themselues into diuers shapes, was
true; shee doth vtterly denie the same, or that euer shee saw
any such practises done by them.
Shee further saith that one Master Thompson, which she
taketh to be Master Christopher Southworth, to whom shee
was sent to learne her prayers, did perswade, counsell, and ad-

uise her to deale as formerly hath beene said against her Grandmother, Aunt, and Southworth's wife.
And further shee confesseth and saith, that shee neuer did
know, or saw any Deuils, nor any other Visions, as formerly by
her hath beene alleaged. Being further demanded whether shee
euer was at Church, shee saith, shee was not, but promised her
after to goe to the Church, and that very willingly.

In the light of this recantation one can only agree with Potts
and applaud the judge's actions. The exposure of a popish plot
seems to have gratified the clerk as much as the discovery of
yet more witches. His attitude to his masters is amusing: clearly
in his eyes they could do no wrong. In the case of the less
fortunate Pendle Witches, Potts had described Jennet Device as
'a young maid whom it had pleased God to raise up' against her
mother. Grace Sowerbutts however, Bromley having detected
her fraud, was 'an impudent wench delivering a strangely de-
vised accusation'. While he never questioned any of Jennet's
charges, he examined Grace's in detail! He drew attention to
the inconsistency between her ill-treatment in the barn and
the consideration shown to her when she went with the women
at night. He could equally well have done this in the case of
Demdike's familiar, Tibb, who did her bidding at times yet at
others pushed her into ditches! He ridiculed the idea that a
woman could turn herself into a dog and in a sentence which
echoes the rationalists of his day rather than King James he
said: 'The wrinkles of an old wiues face is good evidence to the
iurie against a Witch. How often will the common people say
"Her eyes are sunk in her head, GOD bless vs from her".'

Potts was sure of the priest's motive. The three women, he
says, had renounced their allegiance to Rome, and this was his
revenge. Potts suspected that the priest might have been a
Jesuit, a member of the then relatively young but well-disci-
plined order which had made the suppression of heresy one
of its main objects. He rightly accused him of carelessly prepar-
ing his pupil. He had, Potts pointed out, forgotten to devise a

spirit for the three women and had taught the girl out of his own ignorance that it was women themselves who changed their shapes and forms. The 'black things' they met on the banks of the Ribble were obviously priestly invention and the inventor had mistaken the face for the feet. Instead of coaching Grace to say that they were not like men in the face he should have known that it was in being cloven-footed that devils differed from men. Chattox and all her fellow witches agreed about this, he said, referring presumably to her description of Margaret Pearson's familiar. Finally, in closing the case of the 'famous witches of Salmesbury', he blamed the publicity attending the arrest of the Pendle Witches for giving the priest, who already had a motive, both opportunity and encouragement to accuse the poor women and begin to instruct his witness.

One wonders too if the magistrate, Robert Holden, was not encouraged and inspired by the events on the other side of Pendle Hill. To start with, he was married to Alice, daughter of Nicholas Bannister of Altham, and this contact must have kept him well aware of what was afoot; and on just one occasion he is mentioned as sitting with Nowell and Bannister hearing evidence. This evidence, which was read out against Jennet Preston at York, is a short statement by the constable of Pendle Forest, Henry Hargreaves. All he said was that Old Chattox had told him that she knew Preston's wife to be an ill woman who had done great hurt to Master Lister. There is nothing to show where he had this information from Chattox; perhaps Hargreaves escorted the second batch of prisoners to Lancaster and saw her then, possibly enquiring after Jennet Preston on the orders of the justices.

There is no other evidence recorded from this date but the interesting thing is that it was taken before 'Roger Nowell, Nicholas Bannester, and Robert Holden, Esquires, three of his Maiesties Iustices of Peace within the said Countie'. Thus, sitting together on at least one occasion, hearing evidence which concerned Jennet Preston, we find the magistrates involved in

87

the otherwise separate trials of the Pendle Witches, Margaret Pearson and the Witches of Samlesbury.

Isobel Roby

Listed with the Pendle and Samlesbury Witches in the court calendar is the name of a complete stranger—Isobel Roby. She had no connection with any of the others, except that she was tried at the same Assizes and hanged on the same day. She came from Windle near St Helens and was prosecuted by Sir Thomas Gerard, one of the gentlemen who had shown such concern for the welfare of the lame pedlar, John Law. Like other justices he belonged to the gentry of the county—and the Gerrard family were lords of the manor of Windle.

Isobel was charged with having made use of her devilish and wicked arts, but Potts omits to tell us against whom. She seems to have been a poor woman, no longer young, and obviously feared locally. We hear of her begging milk, and of her neighbours turning when they met her in the lane. One young man, who convinced himself that his aches and pains had been wished on him because he had married Isobel's goddaughter, reminds us of Thomas Redfearn. Twice this man appealed for help to counteract the spells under which he was suffering, once to 'James the glover' of Windle, and secondly to 'one Halseworths which they call a wiseman'.

Although it is clear from what he wrote about Alice Nutter that Potts was familiar with James I's *Demonology*, it is in introducing Isobel Roby's trial that he makes his only direct reference to the king's book. 'What,' he asks, 'hath the Kings Maiestie written and published in his Dæmonologie which hath not here beene discouered?' Isobel was found guilty, and although accused of no murder she was sentenced to death. Her crime can be compared with that of the Bulcocks, mother and son, who had driven a woman out of her mind without killing her. Although harsh, her sentence was perfectly in accordance with the Act of 1604 which mentioned those who 'use, practise,

88

or exercise any witchcraft, charm or sorcery, whereby any person shall be killed, destroyed, wasted, pined or lamed in his body'. The death penalty was prescribed for them all.

Isobel Roby's was the last of the witch trials of that particular Assizes and Thomas Potts must have set about compiling his book without delay. The trials ended on 19 August and his account of them was finished by 16 November. Under that date it is obsequiously dedicated by the author to Lord Thomas Knyvet of Escrick in Yorkshire and his 'right honorable and vertvovs ladie, Elizabeth'. The reason for this dedication is not evident although Potts does acknowledge, whatever he may mean by it, that his Lordship's 'Graue and Reuerend Counsell reduced my wauering and wandring thoughts to a more quiet harbour of repose'. The only interest in mentioning Lord Thomas is that he was the man who helped to change the course of English history by discovering Guy Fawkes in the cellars of the palace of Westminster in 1605.

The actual printing of the *Discovery* was done 'by W. Stansby for John Barnes, dwelling near Holborn Conduit' and in a precautionary apology for any printing errors he explains that the work was done 'in such great haste at the end of a Tearme'. Potts' book appears to be a faithful chronicle of the trials, although the author is not against interpolating his own opinions. For instance, he considered Old Demdike to be a 'sink of villainy and mischief', although as she died in prison there was no trial to report and he must never have set eyes on her. In contrast, Chattox's contrition earned his commendation before, in giving his opinions on some of the other accused, he allowed himself to get more inventive and excitable. Elizabeth Device was a 'Barbarous and inhumane Monster', James a 'wicked and miserable wretch', and Anne Redfearn's skill 'in making pictures of clay more cunning than any' qualified her as a 'horrible and bloudie executioner'. Only with Alice Nutter and Katherine Hewitt is there a halt to his flow of invective before he resumes with full force on the Bulcocks 'the most desperate wretches

89

(void of all feare or grace) in all this Packe'. Alizon was an 'odious Witch—able to terrifie and astonish any man liuing', and even Margaret Pearson, whose only crime had been the killing of Dodgson's mare, was considered a 'dangerous Witch of long continuance, little inferiour in her malicious course of life to any that hath gone before'.

Introduced by his own little prefaces, Potts reports the trials in the order in which they occurred, and confessions and pieces of written evidence are chopped up and put into the book piecemeal, according to their relevance to a particular case. Neither the magistrates who wrote them down, the judges, nor their clerk, seem to have been at all concerned by some of the manifest contradictions present in these confessions. Old Chattox, as has been pointed out, could not even be consistent about the place where she had given her soul to the Devil—a memorable event surely, every detail of which we would expect to have been clear even in her old head. Potts calmly records the two quite contradictory accounts of her conversion to witchcraft, the one given to Nowell at Fence, the other told to Covell at Lancaster.

Because of the repetitions and fragmentary presentation of evidence, the contradictions and some obvious mistakes, the *Discovery* is a difficult, albeit fascinating, book from which to extract a lucid account of events. The wording of occasional passages is so hard to interpret that we have had to find consolation in a footnote of Crossley's; he provided notes and observations to the 1845 edition, but when faced with a specially troublesome passage could only comment: 'evidently in so corrupted a state as to bid defiance to any attempt at elucidation.'

Some evidence (notably reports of the meeting at Malkin Tower on Good Friday) Potts repeats again and again, and in doing so illustrates the contemporary lack of concern for consistency in spelling. The famous Tower appears in various places as Maulking, Malking, Malkyn or Malkeing. Most of the book was compiled from documents made available for him to copy, but in recording evidence given in court he must

90

have had extreme difficulty with the barbaric accents of Pendle Forest, and in days when ability to write at all was a rare accomplishment perhaps we should not quibble at these minor variations. We could wish, however, that he had used his time and space to better advantage, giving us in place of the repetitions some of the more intelligent evidence at which he only hints, saying, as in the case of Anne Towneley's husband, that so-and-so was called, but omitting to record the testimony given.

The actual days and months when statements were taken are precisely stated, each piece of testimony being formally headed with name, place and date, copies of what the magistrate had written. For example, the statement of Old Demdike, when she first told of her initiation as a witch is headed:

> The voluntarie Confession and Examination of Elizabeth Sowtherns alias Demdike, taken at the Fence in the Forest of Pendle in the Countie of Lancaster, The second day of Aprill, Annoq; Regni Regis Iacobi Angliæ &c. Decimo, et Scotiæ Quadragesimo quinto; Before Roger Nowell of Reade Esquire, one of his Maiesties Iustices of the peace within the sayd Countie.

Yet there are still errors in this apparent accuracy. We find the eventful month of April 1612, whilst consistently 'Decimo', as in the example just quoted, when applied to James' reign as king of England, put down on successive pages as:

> quadregesimo quarto (44)
> xlv (45)
> xlvj (46), for Scotland.

In just one instance is one of these mistakes disturbing. The piece in question is headed thus:

> The Examination of Alizon Deuice, of the Forrest of Pendle, in the County of Lancaster, Spinster, taken at Reade, in the said Countie of Lancaster, the *xiij.* day of March, Anno Regni Iacobi Angliæ &c. None: et Scotiæ xlv. Before Roger Nowell, etc . . .

The evidence under this date concerns Demdike—it is repeated exactly at Alizon's own trial when Potts says 'it agreeth verbatim with her Examination taken at Reade the thirtieth day of March'.

If the first date could be shown to be true it would mean that enquiries had started before Law was lamed, but as no action was taken against anyone until Abraham Law had made his complaint we have assumed 'xiij' to be a mistake for 30th, under which date the same evidence appears the second time. The 'Anno Regni Jacobi Angliæ None' (ie nine) in this awkwardly dated piece of evidence is explained by the fact that James acceded to the English throne on 24 March. So 13 March was in year nine, 30 March in year ten, of his reign as king of England, yet by Scottish reckoning both were in the forty-fifth year! Although it does not directly affect these dates, until 1 January 1753 the legal year in England began on Lady Day, 25 March, whilst in Scotland, since 1600, they had been celebrating New Year's Day as 1 January. About this time, and well into the eighteenth century, as the two methods of dating seem to have been concurrent in parts of England, dates between 1 January and 24 March are often given a double year. Although Potts did not, someone else might have written 13 March 1611/12 or even 13 March $16\frac{11}{12}$.

In contrast to the vagaries of the confessions, and the evident mistakes in the numbering of the years, no other dates given to the events of 1612 are contradictory, making possible their retelling in correct sequence, and their listing in diary form, in an Appendix (page 171).

On the title-page Potts explained that his book was being 'Published and set forth by commandment of his Maiesties Iustices of Assize for the North Parts.' And when it was finished it was submitted for checking to Judge Bromley. He and his colleague, Altham, must have been gratified to read their clerk's opinion that: 'GOD Almightie had singled out these honourable and reverend judges for the defense of justice in the North Parts.' Little wonder that they declared the account 'carefully set forth . . . truly reported . . . and worthie to be published'.

The book offers as full a record of an English witch trial as any available. Without it the Lancashire Witches would have been no better known than those of Chelmsford or Bury St Edmunds. As it is, thanks to this obscure clerk, and subsequently to the entertaining writings of two novelists, they hold their place as the best-known witches in English history.

CHAPTER V

Other Notable Outbreaks

In 1633 there was another case of supposed witchcraft in Pendle Forest involving more people than the previous one. As in the earlier outbreak much of the evidence accepted was offered by a child, this time a boy of eleven—Edmund Robinson of Wheatley Lane. Ironically Jennet Device, now a woman of about thirty, was amongst the accused.

In view of the multitude of crimes charged against them Roger Nowell can be excused for acting as he did against the witches of his day, but in this later case there seems to be no reason, apart from gross credulity, for the magistrates stirring up another witch-hunt. The account of it reveals the unmindful way in which trials were then conducted, and the callous manner in which prisoners were shown off as one would hesitate nowadays to exhibit animals.

Edmund Robinson's story was this. One night in the autumn of 1633, 1 November to be precise, he was looking for what he called 'bulloes', meaning bullaces—wild plums—when he saw coming towards him two greyhounds, one black, the other brown, each with a string round its neck. He took hold of them but when a hare rose very near and they made no attempt to chase it he began to beat them with a stick he had in his hand, whereupon the black greyhound changed into 'one Dickinson's wife' whom he knew, and the other into a boy, a stranger to him. The woman offered him a shilling, an enormous sum for those days, if he would promise to say nothing of

94

The Examination of Edmund Robinson *Son of* Edmund Robinson *of* Pendle-Foreſt *eleven years of age, taken at* Padham *before* Richard Shutleworth *and* John Starkey *Eſquires, two of his Majeſties Juſtices of the Peace within the County of* Lancaſter, *the* 10th *day of* February, *1633.*

"WHO upon Oath informeth, being examined concerning " the great meeting of the Witches of *Pendle,* ſaith that "upon *All-Saints-day* laſt paſt, he this Informer being " with one *Henry Parker* a near door-neighbour to him in *Wheatley-* " *lane,* deſired the ſaid *Parker* to give him leave to gather ſome "Bulloes which he did ; In gathering whereof he ſaw two Gray- " hounds, *viz.* a black and a brown ; one came running over the " next field towards him, he verily thinking the one of them to be " Mr. *Nutters,* and the other to be Mr. *Robinſons,* the ſaid Gen- " tlemen then having ſuch like. And ſaith, the ſaid Grayhounds " came to him, and fawned on him, they having about their necks " either of them a Collar, unto each of which was tied a ſtring : which " Collars (as this Informer affirmeth) did ſhine like Gold. And he " thinking that ſome either of Mr. *Nutters* or Mr. *Robinſons* Fa- " mily ſhould have followed them ; yet ſeeing no body to follow " them, he took the ſame Gray-hounds thinking to courſe with " them. And preſently a Hare did riſe very near before him. At " the ſight whereof he cried, Loo, Loo, Loo: but the Doggs " would not run. Whereupon he being very angry took them, " and with the ſtrings that were about their Collars, tied them to " a little buſh at the next hedge, and with a ſwitch that he had in " his hand he beat them. And in ſtead of the black Grayhound " one *Dickenſons* Wife ſtood up, a Neighbour whom this Informer " knoweth. And inſtead of the brown one a little Boy, whom this " Informer knoweth not. At which ſight this Informer being a- " fraid, endeavoured to run away : but being ſtayed by the Wo- " man *(viz.)* by *Dickenſons* Wife, ſhe put her hand into her pocket, " and pulled forth a piece of Silver much like to a fair ſhilling, and " offered to give him it to hold his tongue and not to tell : which " he refuſed, ſaying, Nay thou art a Witch. Whereupon ſhe put " her hand into her pocket again, and pulled out a thing like un- " to a Bridle that gingled, which ſhe put on the little Boyes head : " which ſaid Boy ſtood up in the likeneſs of a white Horſe, and in " the brown Grayhounds ſtead. Then immediately *Dickenſons*

Y y 2   ' Wife

the incident, but he made clear his intention of denouncing her as a witch. So she took a bridle from her clothes, put it on the strange boy who by this time had assumed the shape of a white horse, and forced Edmund to ride with her to a place called Hoarstones in Wheatley Lane. (Hoarstones is a large house; in 1633 it was new. Some older maps spell the name as Whorestones, although the early meaning of both versions was probably simply 'white'.)

At this place young Edmund witnessed a gathering of men and women drinking and eating, obtaining some of the meat by pulling on ropes which brought lumps of butter and smoking flesh down from the ceiling to fall into basins. He also claimed to have seen three women take down from the beams three clay pictures stuck full of thorns. He got away without much difficulty although he said he was followed by two of the witches. These were eventually frightened off when they encountered two horsemen at a place ominously named Boggart Hole. (A 'boggart' is a ghost in the local dialect.)

Edmund's father, also called Edmund, was a poor man described as a waller or mason. He said that he had found his son in a distressed state after his experiences, but that when he had recovered the lad told him the tale as it was now being told to the magistrates. The evidence was taken down at Padiham, an unexplained three months after the incident. The magistrates were Richard Shuttleworth of Gawthorpe and John Starkie of Huntroyd. As a consequence of the imaginings of young Edmund a large number of suspects was rounded up, taken to Lancaster and tried. Seventeen were found guilty by the jury. The comparative shambles of a seventeenth-century courtroom compared with the decorous scene today is revealed by the complaint of one of the accused at this trial, who said later that she had been unable to answer for herself in court because she was prevented by the noise of the crowd from hearing the evidence offered against her.

Instead of the guilty being next day carried to the place of execution and hanged, a report of the trial was sent to the king, Charles I, and his Privy Council, in London. They instructed Henry Bridgeman, Bishop of Chester, to examine some of the women (Pendle Forest was then in the diocese of Chester), but before the bishop could report it had been requested that four of them should be sent to London. These four were lodged at the Ship Tavern at Greenwich, near to one of the royal residences, and were examined by numerous surgeons and midwives and later by the king himself. Amongst the surgeons was William Harvey, famous for first demonstrating the circulation of the blood. This medical jury issued a certificate on 2 July 1635 which said:

> We have inspected the bodies of Jennet Hargreaves, Frances Dickinson, and Mary Spencer, and have found nothing unnatural, nor anything like a teat or mark. There was nothing on the body of Margaret Johnson inconsistent with a well known disease.

Margaret Johnson, a widow of about sixty, had nevertheless made a classic confession of her guilt, stating precisely how, when, where, and for what purpose she had, of her own free will, become a witch.

Times were changing, although there were to be notable relapses, for during the twenty-four years of the reign of Charles I only six executions for witchcraft are recorded. The fate of the reprieved witches is somewhat in doubt, and some of those originally accused were still being held at Lancaster three years after the trial. In the accounts we have of this trial there is an interesting mention of Jennet Device having a half-brother— William Device. Nothing more is known about him or his parentage; he was certainly never mentioned by Potts.

Following the trial Edmund Robinson had been set up as a witch-finder by his father and uncle. This unscrupulous pair took the boy around to Sunday services in churches in the locality, where he proceeded to detect witches in the congregation. Just how, short of blackmail, the two men turned the boy's act into profit is not clear, but it is known that his father, until then a poor man, was by this enabled to buy himself a couple of cows. However, their reign was short. The boy and his mentors were themselves summoned to London and separated. Young Edmund then admitted that his original story was entirely false, that he had been put up to telling it by his father and encouraged by him to continue after the trial. We do not know what happened to the men but Edmund the boy returned to live out his life in his native village.

There was no Thomas Potts to publish an account of this trial and for the information about it we have to depend on the accounts, which do not vary significantly, in Whitaker's *History of Whalley* or Baines' *History of Lancaster*, and on a third, the most interesting and original source, John Webster's *Displaying of Supposed Witchcraft*. Webster was born in 1610 in the hamlet of Thornton, in the parish of Coxwold, Yorkshire. In 1634 he was curate of Kildwick in Craven, and in 1643 master of the Grammar School at Clitheroe. He was at some time a chaplain in the army and admits to having practised the art of medicine. His connection with the witch-finding Robinsons is well explained in his own words:

> [Edmund Robinson] was brought into the church at Kildwick where I, being then curate there, was preaching in the afternoon, and was set upon a stool to look about him, which moved some little disturbance in the congregation for a while. After prayers I enquired what the matter was; the people told me it was the boy that discovered witches; upon which I went to the house where he was to stay all night, and here I found him and two very unlikely persons, that did conduct him and manage the business. I desired to have some discourse with the boy in private, but that was utterly refused. Then, in the presence of a great many people, I took the boy near me and said: 'Good boy, tell me truly and in earnest, didst thou see and hear such strange things at the meeting of witches as is reported by many thou didst relate?' But the two men, not giving the boy leave to answer, did pluck him from me, and said he had been examined by two able justices of the peace, and they did never ask him such a question.

This was in 1634. In his book, not published until 1677, Webster tells us that Edmund, the youthful source of all the trouble those forty years before, was still living at Wheatley Lane. He was by then better known by his nickname 'Ned o' Roughs' and was fond of recounting the mischievous and dishonourable activities of his boyhood. Webster's book gives a good account of the trial which must have been another sensation for the county and this time for London too, for we learn that the four women sent to the capital were put on show at the Fleet Prison—'great sums gotten at the Fleet to show them, public plays acted thereupon'. One of the plays to which Webster refers was titled *The Late Lancashire Witches*. Its authors, Thomas Heywood and Richard Brame, must have worked fast, as it was being acted at the Globe Theatre, Bankside, in 1634! A much later play by Shadwell, *The Lancashire Witches*, produced in 1682, mixes up the characters and events from both 1612 and 1633 trials.

By the time Webster came to publish his book belief in witches was declining, but his opinions are so illuminating that we have made much use of them when the rights and wrongs of the cases are discussed.

John Webster came into contact, personally, as a young curate, with a family of rather amateur witch-finders. We do not know what branch of his versatile career he was following, clergyman, teacher, physician or soldier, when England's most professional witch-hunter became briefly famous. Matthew Hopkins, the self-styled 'Witchfinder General', was the only individual in English history whose number of victims puts him in the same class as some of the continental fanatics. Although he lived in another part of the kingdom, and was active some years later than the Lancashire Witches, some account of him cannot be left out of any book of English witch trials.

A minister's son, Hopkins was a lawyer, 'but of little note', in Ipswich. From whence he removed to Maningtree, where he accused a poor one-legged woman called Elizabeth Clarke of being a witch. This accusation began a process which snow-balled into a trial at Chelmsford where eighteen were hanged. This was in 1645, and in a time of Civil War this energetic rogue and his partner, a man called Stearne, seem to have got away with practices which had not before been tolerated. Hopkins it was who advocated, and practised, the stripping and trussing of suspects, who were then watched for at least twenty-four hours to see if they were visited by their familiars, or imps, and a creature as small as a spider was interpreted as an imp. Another form of the 'hard usage and questions' which he advocated was the 'walking' and enforced wakefulness, after three days of which his victims were willing to confess to anything to obtain relief. At the height of their brief power these two rogues employed as many as four assistants, all considered expert in the pricking and swimming of witches. They visited towns in Essex, Suffolk and neighbouring counties, either at their own initiative, or by invitation. They expected their keep and commanded a fee of twenty shillings for every detected witch—a rare inducement to find them. Hopkins was responsible for the conviction of the only Church of England clergyman who, so far as we are aware, was executed as a witch. Parson Lowis, or Lewis, vicar of Brandeston in Suffolk for fifty years, was at the age of seventy accused of witchcraft, and had the misfortune to be interrogated by Hopkins, whose partner, Stearne, left an account of the case.

According to him Lowis confessed to covenanting with the Devil and sealing the pact with blood. He admitted to having three imps which sucked at the marks found on his body, and he claimed he had been able, with the help of his yellow imp, when standing by the sea, to pick out a ship from a small fleet which was sailing by, raise a sudden boisterous storm round this particular vessel and thereby sink it. All these admissions are explained when we read Stearne's ominous statement: 'Mr Hopkins took his confession.' From another source we discover how this was done:

Lowis stoutly maintained his innocence and challenged his accusers to prove their charges, so they kept him awake several nights together and ran him backwards and forwards about the room until he was out of breath. They rested him a little then ran him again till he was weary of his life and scarce sensible of what he said or did.

Lowis was one of those hanged in 1645 in Bury St Edmunds, and being naturally desirous of a Christian burial he read the office himself, committing his own soul to the care of his maker. Another of Hopkins' victims was burnt to death at Ipswich (Mother Lakeland, 9 September 1645), but she had used witchcraft to do away with her husband, and as this was petty treason the penalty was burning.

Records of the trials which followed in Hopkins' wake are lost or incomplete, and so figures will never be accurately known, but it seems probable that Hopkins and Stearne, in the two short years of their reign, were responsible for the hanging, or burning, as in the case just cited, of nearly three hundred witches. Parliament, after appeal had been made to it, finally put a stop to their evil work by appointing a special commission to limit their activities. Soon after this the judges at Norfolk Assizes were accusing Hopkins of practising all sorts of cruelties and fleecing the country for his own profit. And so this man, who at one time claimed to have the Devil's list of all the witches in England, had his reign of terror cut short. He retired to Maningtree and within a year died, not as is so often reported by being himself swum as a suspected witch, but from tuberculosis.

Belief in witchcraft had not unnaturally crossed the ocean with the early settlers in America, and the Puritan mind was particularly tuned to detect the workings of the Devil. One of the most dreadful cases where children pretended, in the presence of certain adults, to fall into uncontrollable fits, occurred at Salem in Massachusetts, in 1692. The demented behaviour of a group of girls was diagnosed by the local ministers and physician as due to witchcraft. The girls' ages ranged from twelve to twenty—teenagers, living for kicks in a much more disastrous and cruel manner than their modern sisters, and revelling in the awful consequences of their counterfeited behaviour. 'We must have sport,' one of them admitted later.

In all, one hundred and fifty people were eventually accused of being witches, and a strange feature of the case was the acquittal of the fifty or so who decided to confess. Amongst the crueller incidents was the binding of some suspects at the heels and neck until the blood oozed from their noses, and the chaining of a little girl of five, Dorothy Good, in the dungeon with her mother. The woman was hanged and the child permanently deranged by the experience. Evidence was accepted from a seven-year-old, the hangman's fees were charged to relatives, and the accused, even if acquitted, had to pay for their keep in gaol. The district must have gone mad and one bizarre occurrence was the solemn trial and hanging of a wretched dog for his part in the proceedings!

Fortunately the workings of the law took time. Thirty-one were brought to trial in 1692, of whom nineteen were hanged. Two died in gaol and one was executed by the then legal method of 'pressing to death'. Victims who had refused to plead were stretched on the ground, a board was put on top, and heavy weights were heaped on this. By the next year evidence which had been freely allowed in the first trials was being declared unacceptable, and no more hangings took place. In 1696 the twelve jurors at the first trial published a confession of error and a few years later an inadequate sum of six hundred pounds was distributed as reimbursement for the families of those wrongly hanged.

Like so many witch trials it was well reported. Cotton Mather's *Wonders of the Invisible World*, published in Boston in 1693, gave a good account of the trials and the events surrounding them. In recent years Arthur Miller's play *The Crucible* has retold the story, dramatically displaying the processes by which a combination of mistaken beliefs and mischief filled this New England village with suspicion and fear.

CHAPTER VI

The Continental Influence

IT is an obvious conclusion from all witch trials, whether in
Lancashire, America or anywhere else, that these unfortunates
who were hanged or pilloried, or who suffered long degrading
months in dungeons before eventual release, were, despite any
confessions which might have been coaxed from them, credited
with powers they never possessed, and were innocent of the
harm they were considered to have done.

Although today, as ever, there are daily and world-wide mani-
festations of evil, few people attribute these to the workings of
Satan. Fewer still, even amongst those who credit his existence,
would be prepared to believe that he, or any of his legion of
minor demons, ever appeared on earth to be worshipped or
consulted by the Demdikes and Chattoxes, or any of the hundreds of similar women and men with whom he was supposed
to have made his covenant.

The evils generated in such places as Pendle Forest, the
deaths, the strokes, the ailments of cattle, were obviously natural.
Nowadays they would be diagnosed and dealt with as such.
But we have far more understanding of disease and other
natural phenomena than previous centuries possessed. From
our relative wisdom we should look back with sympathy at the
ignorance of our forbears. Since man walked the earth he has
been aware of forces whose operation he could not understand
and has continually tried to command or influence these. His

way was to utter spells or perform rites, use charms, or invoke the aid of the spirit world in which he firmly believed, or use the sort of imitative magic practised by primitive man to this day—as when one of the tribe acts the part of the prey and by being deliberately caught hopes to ensure the success of the hunt that is to follow.

As the doctors and scientists of their day, magicians and sorcerers, the students or supposed masters of supernatural forces, have in different times and in different places been officially employed or officially condemned. The Old Testament contains many examples of sacred magic, but whilst King Nebuchadnezzar 'commanded to call the magicians, and the enchanters, and the sorcerers' to interpret his dreams, King Saul, having cast the fortune-tellers and necromancers out of his kingdom, had to consult in secret the woman of Endor. Magicians in England led a precarious life. The services of the most famous of them, John Dee, were once sought by Queen Elizabeth, when a wax image of her, impaled through the breast with a pin, was found in Lincoln's Inn Fields. The same Dr Dee had been imprisoned by Queen Mary, and in later life he asked to be publicly tried to clear his name of repeated accusations of evil practices.

Magic, although the word is often loosely used, was considered to be a science which could produce results without the aid of spirits. Sorcery, on the other hand, was worked with spirits 'conjured' up to help the sorcerer. The word 'conjurer' was formally applied to an invoker of evil spirits. As the appearance of these was, to say the least, extremely uncertain, conjurers often resorted to the sort of tricks we expect from those who nowadays bear the name.

An amalgamation of all these ignorant ideas about illness, magic and sorcery could account for the sort of persecution we have described, and the impression gained from accounts such as Potts' *Discovery* is that English witch trials were the final cruel manifestation of the unenlightened and superstitious beliefs of

104

the time. The truth is much more sinister. English witch-hunting can be understood, not by examining bucolic superstitions, but only by studying the sophisticated doctrine of witchcraft which for three hundred years imposed itself on Europe—on France and the various states which now comprise Germany, in particular.

If dates are wanted, we can take the three centuries from about 1450 to 1750 as the limits of the persecution. It reached a climax about 1600, at the beginning of what has been well described as a 'peculiarly persecuting century'. During this time many thousands of supposed witches were cruelly and painfully put to death. We shall never know the number who perished, and might have found even the most modest estimates hard to credit, had we not witnessed in our own times another terrible persecution of innocent people: the Nazis' attempted extermination of the Jews. It was more concentrated than the campaign against the witches, but was probably no more terrible in terms of human suffering.

There are points of resemblance between the two. Both were presented as 'purifying' operations, an attempt by an authority, which supposedly knew best, to rid the people of an evil. Laws were not broken, but were altered to give power to the persecutors. Local authorities, who might have remained lukewarm, were guided and encouraged by trained fanatics appointed by the central power; in the case of the Jews, the Nazi party; in the case of the witches, the Christian Church.

In both campaigns, against witches and Jews, property was confiscated, and ordinary citizens intimidated until, through fear of losing their own freedom and lives, they dare not give help, or sign of support, to the oppressed, or speak out against the oppressors. The knowledge that even in the twentieth century a cultured nation can be led to commit and condone atrocities, helps us to appreciate the madness which afflicted our forbears in parts of the continent and which spread, in a fortunately much diluted form, to England. When compared with countries abroad English witch-hunts were mild, humane and few in number.

When Christianity was adopted by Constantine and became the official religion of the Roman Empire, the Church set about the enemies which threatened its unity with all the vigour with which the early Christians had themselves been assailed. By the fourth century, in parts of Europe, heresy was already punishable by death, although the laws do not seem to have been actively enforced.

Bishops were ordered to look for deviations from the officially proclaimed truth and to stem the progress of these errors. When these local enquiries proved insufficient Pope Innocent III appointed inquisitors directly from Rome. Papal power was such in those days that the secular authorities, to whom the Church's victims were delivered for punishment, could be made to promise on oath 'to exterminate from the land all heretics who have been marked by the Church'. As with everything the Church did, justification could be found for this heresy-hunting in the Bible:

> If thy brother . . . entice thee secretly saying Let us go and serve other Gods . . . thou shalt not consent unto him . . . neither shall thine eye pity him, neither shalt thou spare, neither shalt thou conceal him, but thou shalt surely kill him . . . and all Israel shall hear and fear and shall do no more any such wickedness. . . .

> If thou shalt hear tell concerning one of thy cities, saying, Certain base fellows have . . . drawn away the inhabitants . . . saying Let us go and serve other gods . . . then shalt thou enquire, and make search, and ask diligently . . . and if it be truth that such abomination is wrought in the midst of thee, thou shalt surely smite the inhabitants of that city.
>
> (Deuteronomy 13)

It was to direct the killing and smiting that the Inquisition was created. With misguided sincerity it tortured and burnt its way through Europe, and the colonies of Asia and America particularly, for the next five hundred years. So far as the hounding of witches was concerned, the Protestants, in those parts where they gained power following the Reformation, must share the responsibility. Lutherans and Calvinists did not hesitate to adopt the theories of the Church of Rome and were equally zealous and cruel in applying them.

The idea of a witch such as King James defined took a long time to develop. Originally the word applied to a man or woman with magical powers, usually evil, and this uncomplicated idea was pre-Christian. From very early times it had been believed that there were women with the ability to fly through the air on sticks, change their human form into that of an animal, bring down hail which could ruin crops, and raise storms which could sink ships. The new witches against whom the Church was joining battle were still credited with these legendary powers. What was novel was the introduction of the Devil into their rites, and the stories of their periodical assemblies to do him homage. On the Continent, and in Scotland, witches were tortured until they confessed to all these absurd activities. Their confessions were then regarded both as evidence of their guilt and as confirmation of the reality of their crimes.

Until the thirteenth century the Church officially considered the traditional powers of witches as imaginary, bred of insanity or dreams. It was therefore heretical to express belief in their reality. A canon of uncertain origin, usually referred to as the 'Canon Episcopi', was often quoted in support of this earlier, more enlightened view. As a part of Church dogma, it could not be ignored by the new generation of theologians, those who sought to convince people that intercourse with Satan, lycanthropy and night-flying were not imaginings but facts. Some, like Thomas Aquinas, denied the canon, others accepted it but declared that even if existing in the imagination only, such beliefs were dangerous, meriting death and justifying torture.

Yet another way round it was argue that a different breed

of witches had come into being since it was formulated—not an unreasonable argument, perhaps comparable with present-day medical beliefs that the ineffectiveness of certain treatments is due to the perverse mutations of the particular germ or virus under attack. The witchcraft the inquisitors were fighting was declared by some to be a different thing, connected only in name with the old country superstitions condemned as imaginary by the Canon Episcopi.

The idea of the Devil as the embodiment of all evil, and the arch-enemy of God, was itself an amalgam of earlier ideas—ideas gradually brought together to form the picture of the horned, cloven-footed, fork-tailed father of lies we picture today. His functions as an enemy of good Christians are well described in the abusive names by which he was addressed by the exorcists: 'Master of the worst actions; chief of accursed murder; author of incest; head of sacrilege; inventor of all obscenities; teacher of heretics.' He was called by many names—Satan, Lucifer, Beelzebub—and although these once referred to different entities, for our purpose they can be considered interchangeable. Belief in his existence, if not acceptance of his appearance, is still part of the faith of many.

The work started by the Church was soon shared by laymen —lawyers and magistrates, encouraged or tolerated, very rarely opposed, by the bishops and princes under whom they lived. The pattern of savage persecution was established early. The Inquisition's first major campaign was against an heretical sect called the Cathars, which flourished in France in the twelfth and thirteenth centuries. A holy war was preached against these people, who, out of hostility to their corrupt clergy, had developed a brand of Christianity which laid particular stress on personal behaviour. After a long and bitter crusade the Cathars were wiped out, with the same exceptional cruelties of torture and mass burnings which were to become a feature with the Inquisition's next victims—the witches.

In the three hundred years that followed, many thousands of

words were written, and many more thousands spoken, in debating the relationship between sorcery and heresy, and the part played by the Devil in these activities: and during this period, when the doctrines of witchcraft were taking shape in the minds of inquisitors and judges, there was much learned debate about God's motive in allowing his enemy to work so much evil.

So the new dogma grew, consisting of elements from primitive superstition, sorcery and ritual magic, the whole built round the covenant with the Devil. In Eastern Europe where the Church was, as now, separate from Rome, nobody thought to formulate such a system, although the same beliefs in magic, night-flying, vampirism and so on were as strongly held as elsewhere, had anyone cared to weld them together into a new heresy and put the Devil at its head. In Western Europe the new doctrine was confirmed by thousands of unfortunate victims, men and women who probably believed in the reality of witchcraft and were afraid of witches, but who had never bargained on being themselves suspected. In order to instruct the uninitiated in the evil mysteries of the new heresy many books were written, culminating, about 1486, in the first publication of the most notorious of all books on witchcraft, the *Malleus Maleficarum*.

On 9 December 1484, Pope Innocent VIII, 'servant of the servants of God' as he styled himself, issued a bull expressing his deep concern at the abominable practices, recently brought to his notice, in which so-called Christians, particularly in parts of North Germany, were indulging.

> Many persons of both sexes, unmindful of their own salvation and deviating from the Catholic faith, have abandoned themselves to devils, and by their incantations, spells, conjurations and horrid charms destroy children, cattle and crops; torment men and women with pain and disease; hinder men from generating and women from conceiving; blasphemously renounce that faith which they received by the sacrament of baptism; and at the instigation of the Devil commit the foulest abominations and excesses, to the peril of their souls.

He went on to complain that his two delegated inquisitors in those parts of Germany—Heinrich Kramer and Jakob Sprenger —had met denials by the local authorities that these enormities were practised. This, he thought, was because the abominations they were seeking had not been described in sufficient detail and therefore went unrecognised. The Pope then continued:

> We decree and enjoin that the aforesaid Inquisitors be empowered to proceed to the just correction, imprisonment and punishment of any persons, of whatever rank and high estate, correcting, mulcting, imprisoning, punishing as their crimes merit, those whom they have found guilty. They are authorised to call on the help of the secular arm, and anyone, of whatever rank, pre-eminence or dignity who opposes them is threatened with excommunication, and yet more terrible penalties and punishments without any right of appeal.

With the backing of the Pope, Kramer and Sprenger, two Dominicans renowned as preachers and scholars, set down in detail, in the quarter of a million words in the *Malleus Maleficarum*, all they could find out of witchcraft. The Latin title of the book can be translated as the 'Hammer of Evil'; the weapon, that is, with which this heresy was to be recognised and crushed. We shall refer to it henceforward, for the sake of brevity, as the *Malleus*.

The book is in three parts. The first discusses the relationship between the Devil and witches and seeks to explain why God should ever tolerate such a conspiracy. The second describes what witches do and how their evil may be countered, and the last explains the procedures for their trial and punishment. The *Malleus* listed the witches' crimes against men and the Church, and gave intimate details of the sexual connections between humans and devils—men with succubi, the female demons; women with incubi, the male species. It gave detailed instructions to judges as to the proper procedure at trials, and it authorised torture to obtain confessions. It did not begin the persecution, otherwise its authors would not have been able to

cite instances of witch-burning, but it codified the new teachings and reversed the process by which the Church had been
slowly condemning and discarding old, ignorant ideas, and it
condemned as heretics any who were not prepared to join the
battle against the Devil and his human minions.

Parts of it can be traced to earlier books, but it is without
doubt the most influential book on witchcraft ever written. It has
been reprinted several times within recent years and one of
these editions has an introduction by the Rev Montague Summers, himself a firm believer in witchcraft and the reality of
the Devil. He is entitled to talk about its 'seemingly inexhaustible
wells of wisdom in which later writers drew' and to describe it
as 'that very great and very wise book'. To most of us today it
seems an evil book which gave the Church's blessing to the
torturers, and caused centuries of unnecessary suffering. It is a
book in which logic, common sense and compassion are lacking,
and in which the authors, anticipating some types of modern
journalism, seem to dwell over-long on the details of the supposed sex life of the witches and the anatomy of the devils who
satisfied their lusts. It came at a time when the development of
printing was making books more readily available. At least
fourteen editions were printed between 1486 and 1520, and,
starting in 1584, at least six editions were put out in English.
To quote the introduction to a recent edition: 'The Malleus
lay on the bench of every judge and on the desk of every magistrate—it was the ultimate, irrefutable, unarguable authority.'
It was the book from which, as one sixteenth-century author
wrote, 'all the authors that ever I have read do receive their
light, authority and arguments,' and although the imaginary
evils which it was combating are called sorcery, devil worship,
or witchcraft, the word most commonly used for the Devil's
agents, for whose downfall the book was written, is 'witches'.

The authors of the *Malleus* had complained of the hostility
and apathy which met them; and the Pope's strongly-worded
order was put out to remove the hindrances to their work.

Although the common people of Europe believed in magic and sorcery, they gave little encouragement to the witch-hunters. Hence the need, if the mass of the people was to be made to support the opinion of the Church, for sermons to convince the illiterate, books to inform those who could read and public confessions to precede the public burnings.

The gradual growth of the witch-persecution was ascribed by the persecutors to the increased activity of the Devil. It was, in fact, due to the increased activity of the witch-hunters, each generation of whom took over and elaborated the theories of the previous one; and each theory, which would not have stood up against the least breath of common sense, was confirmed in the terror and torment of the torture chamber. In those areas where it took hold, witches were held responsible for every misfortune. Some German towns—an example is Bamberg—had a special witch-prison or 'Hexenhaus'. Magistrates and judges, urged to do something and faced with the task of proving an impossible crime, turned for instruction to such books as the *Malleus*. The principal crime was no longer the harming of one's neighbour, but the holding of heretical beliefs. It was written 'this indeed is the end of all witchcraft, that there should be a contract with the Devil, by which contract the witch binds herself to be a servant of the Devil, and devotes herself to him'. The sort of witchcraft described was, therefore, confined to Christian countries. It had to be, since heresy is a crime against the Church.

Whilst France and Germany suffered most, surprisingly Spain, which either at home or in its colonies has over the years burnt more than its share of heretics, was relatively free from witch-hunts. There were some burnings; but the spread of the delusion was halted about the time of the Lancashire Witches, when the Central Committee of the Inquisition, which was a national institution in Spain and therefore not controlled from Rome, wisely accepted the findings of Alonzo de Salazar y Frias, a judge who in 1610 had been involved in the trials of

Basque witches. After a thorough enquiry following the trials, amongst a large number of witches who, be it noted, had already confessed to their crimes, he reported that he had found no evidence that a single act of witchcraft had occurred. Thereafter, in witch trials, normal laws of evidence were insisted upon, confiscation of property was very much restricted and witchcraft in Spain came almost to an end.

Elsewhere it was admitted by lawyers that not one in a thousand witches would be convicted if regular legal procedures were followed. So, as witchcraft was such an exceptional crime, and as the witches could supposedly count on the invisible aid of that master of cunning, the Devil, many normal processes of law were put to one side. Rumour or gossip about a man or woman, an accusation forced out of a prisoner by torture, or a false promise of pardon, were all accepted as evidence of guilt. Trials for witchcraft seem to have been designed to display the details of the crime for which the accused was already assumed to be guilty, rather than to establish her guilt or innocence.

A witch trial could be instigated if someone went before a judge, accused a person of heresy, or of protecting heretics, and was prepared to prove his case. But the *Malleus* even gave authority for a trial to begin when the accuser did not offer to bring evidence to support his charge, but merely stated that he laid the information out of zeal for the faith. A third method of initiating a trial involved an inquisition, following a general report that there were witches in some town or place. To quote the *Malleus*:

> Let the judge take note that he is not bound to publish the names of the accusers, or to bring them before the accused. In considering the method of proceeding with the trial of a witch, such cases must be conducted in the simplest and most summary manner, without the arguments and contentions of advocates.

And lastly:

> Note that persons under sentence of excommunication, notorious

evil-doers and criminals, are admitted as witnesses in a case concerning the faith, and just as a heretic may give evidence against a heretic, so may a witch against a witch.

A French lawyer, Henri Boguet, who was alive in 1612, was writing: 'In this crime the judge should not even reject the evidence of children who have not yet reached the age of puberty.' And his fellow-countryman and contemporary, Jean Bodin, was torturing children to get them to testify against their parents.

All the suggested alterations in the normal methods of conducting trials were justified by long arguments. It was contended, for instance, that it was dangerous to make known the names of her accusers to a person who was bound to have so many evil accomplices still at liberty, and besides absolving the judge from the duty of publishing the names, anyone connected with the trial was forbidden, under pain of excommunication, to reveal them or to tell any secrets they had learned from the inquisitors. The accused was not allowed to choose her own advocate. If an advocate was chosen by the judge he could refuse or abandon the case and the *Malleus* warned that he himself could be charged with defending heresy and stood in danger of excommunication. It will be understood therefore, that it was very rare for any sort of case to be allowed on behalf of the accused.

When a trial or enquiry started in a town there were judges, scribes, guards and torturers to pay and feed; and since these costs were met from the confiscated property of the condemned, it was essential to condemn someone. And since, after confessing, every witch was again tortured until she gave a list of accomplices, the supply of victims was constant. Once established, a persecution of this kind kept itself going. Men, women and children confessed under torture to their dealings with the Devil. Children as young as seven went to the stake. From the custom of confiscating property, the rich were if anything in greater peril than the poor. The atmosphere of dread and mistrust that must have prevailed is well conveyed in a letter written three hundred years ago by a village priest who lived near Bonn. 'Professors, law students, pastors, canons, vicars and monks are being arrested and burnt. One does not know with what people one may talk or associate.'

Torture as a means of discovering heresy had the sanction of the Church and was not officially proscribed as a method of persuasion until 1816. The *Malleus* said:

> The accused should be stripped, if a woman by a jury of matrons, the purpose of this stripping is to discover whether she should have hidden upon her body some charm which would enable her to withstand the torture. Some hide them in their hair, others in the more secret parts of their bodies.

One can well imagine the licence this latter suggestion would give to men with the mentality of the gaolers; and although women were supposed to be stripped by women, 'upright and of good character', in one case at least there is clear evidence to show that the victim was raped by the torturers at this stage, and it is very unlikely that this proven example of abuse was an isolated one. In England as we have seen, the stripping of suspects had a rather different purpose to the one mentioned here. It was not for finding hidden charms in unmentionable crevices, but for the discovery of some witch's mark or teat, or the insensitive Devil's mark.

After searching, the accused was shown the torture chamber, and the instruments prepared for use on her, and exhorted to confess. Then, to quote the *Malleus*:

> The next action of the judge is clear, for as common justice demands that a witch should not be convicted except on her own confession, she must be exposed to questions and torture to extort a confession of her crimes. If, after being fittingly tortured, she still refuses to confess the truth, the judge shall have other engines of torture brought before her and tell her that she will have to endure these.

The methods of torture varied from place to place, and from torturer to torturer. To take an example of which we have details, in Germany one day in 1629, one woman had her hair burnt off at the roots (accomplished by throwing alcohol over it and setting the spirit alight), her hands were tied behind her back and she was left hanging from the ceiling for three hours. During this time her tormentors had breakfast. Heavy weights were then hung on her body and she was jerked up and down. Her thumbs, toes and legs were squeezed in vices and she was whipped until she bled. This torture was alternated with questioning and, as she held out, it was started all over again on the next day. Consecrated salt and blessed herbs were recommended for use in the torture chamber to protect those involved from harm and as a further precaution many of the instruments used to crush the victim's limbs or tear her flesh bore three little marks representing the Trinity.

Whipping, the use of thumbscrews, stretching on the rack and some other torments were regarded as preliminaries; confessions at this stage were often recorded as 'voluntary' or 'without torture'. We have first-hand confirmation of this: a Father von Spee, a Jesuit priest, and one of the few of his kind who protested against the persecution of witches, wrote:

> Judges frequently record that the accused has confessed without torture. I inquired into this and learnt that in reality they were tortured, but only in an iron press with sharp-edged channels over the shins. In this they were pressed like a cake, bringing blood and causing intolerable pain, and this is technically called 'without torture', deceiving those who do not understand the phrases of the inquisitors.

The human mind has a comforting habit of forgetting the horrors of the past or even turning them into items of comedy. We joke about being 'thrown to the lions' or 'hanged, drawn and quartered'. Rascally pirates and brutish highwaymen are transmuted into heroes or figures of fun, and on the stage even a torturer in W. S. Gilbert's flippant hands emerges as a pathetic rather than frightening figure. But now and again in any serious enquiry the truth must be faced. And the truth was, in the days of the continental witch-hunts, that torturing was a trade. Evidence of this can be found in a remarkable document reprinted in Rossell Hope Robbins' *Encyclopedia of Witchcraft and Demonology* (the original is in the library of Cornell University). This remarkable 'Tariff of Torture' lists forty-nine items and the charge for each. Comparisons with current fees are difficult, but cutting out the tongue and burning the mouth with a red-hot iron was considered by the Archbishop of Cologne, who authorised the charges, to merit five times the reward for flogging a prisoner in gaol. Other items read:

For terrorising and showing the instruments of torture	1 Thaler
For arranging and crushing the thumbs for the first degree of torture	¼ Thaler
For the second degree of torture, including setting the limbs afterwards	2¼ Thalers

Those in charge of tortures and executions were instructed to 'submit afterwards their accounts, with all their vouchers, to the Treasury of the Archbishop'. And in an instruction which should delight the heart of any good trade unionist, it is made clear that 'only the executioner, and no stranger, shall be employed for whatever executions have to be done'. All these costs formed part of the heavy expenses of a trial and had to be paid eventually by the family of the accused.

So the explanation of the ridiculous confessions is horribly simple. Unendurable pain sooner or later forced supposed agents of the Devil to assent to anything suggested to them by the scribe who sat at the torturer's side. One woman told her confessor before she died that she never dreamt that suffering could force a person to tell such lies as she had told; confided that she was not a witch and had never seen the Devil. She had been forced eventually to plead guilty and accuse others, thus exposing herself to the eternal damnation in which as a Christian she believed, and which she hoped her dying confession would avert.

From the similarity of many confessions it seems that a form, or order, of questioning was common to many areas, and that in some cases the accused had only to answer 'yes' to the suggestions of her tormentors. These were then written down in the first person and read out to the crowd at the execution. If, when the torment was eased, victims went back on their admissions, they were again taken to the torture chamber. Their eventual fate was not altered but they would be more than likely burnt alive, and spared the mercy of being strangled before the fire was lit. Very few resisted for long, although one incredible case is on record of a woman who was tortured on fifty-six occasions but refused to confess.

The stereotyped questions usually elucidated the length of time the accused had been a witch; the details of the witches' meetings she had attended, and how she had travelled to them; the harm she had done to people, animals and crops, the storms she had raised; and the number of times she had had intercourse with the Devil or with minor demons, with very often intimate details of this intercourse.

Henri Boguet, the French lawyer (whose opinions on the evidence of children we have just quoted), came to be considered an authority on witchcraft. His book *Discourses on Sorcery* rivalled the *Malleus* and ran to twelve editions in its first twenty years. It was based on his own experience at witch trials and his description of the various practices attributed to witches may be taken as stating the popular belief of his time— the late sixteenth and early seventeenth centuries. He is less long-winded and tortuous than the authors of the *Malleus* and describes a witch-meeting or Sabbat thus:

The witches, being assembled, first worship Satan, who appears to them now in the shape of a big black man and now as a goat, and to do him the greater homage they kiss him on the shameful parts behind. Following this they dance in a ring back to back, there are also demons which join in these dances. After the dancing the witches begin to couple with each other, and in this matter the son does not spare his mother, nor the brother his sister, nor the father his daughter. After having abandoned themselves to such foul, fleshly pleasures, they fall to feasting and banqueting, before rendering to Satan an account of what they have done since the last assembly. Those are most welcome who have caused the death of most persons or cattle, or have cast the most spells of illness.

The plight of any person on whom one of these spells had been put was indeed pitiable, as these further extracts from Boguet show:

Witches cause him whom they have bewitched to void, sometimes from the mouth and sometimes from the bottom parts, needles, hairs, stones and papers. I myself have seen an infinite number of such articles, amongst them balls, locks of hair and pig's bristles.

He goes on to give an account which he had 'from a gentleman who may be believed': 'Some time ago, one of his sons voided by the penis five or six paper notes and some peas. The notes were covered in strange characters and the peas were wrapped in hair.' When a bewitched girl was cured, '. . . the Devils came out of her mouth in the shape of balls as big as a fist and red as fire. When all these Devils had come out they danced three or four times round the fire and then vanished.' The girl, he laconically reports, then began to recover her health. Little wonder!

The idea of the broomstick as the very symbol of a witch had not then developed. It was present, but not particularly prominent. Boguet quotes from a witch's confession in which she says that to go to the Sabbat 'she placed a white staff between her legs and uttered certain words, and was then conveyed through the air to the assembly'. Others, she said 'sometimes went on horses, sometimes astride brooms'. In one of his pictures the sixteenth-century Flemish painter Brueghel shows a witch astride a baker's peel—the long wooden shovel used for taking bread out of hot ovens. Belief in a witch's ability to fly was easily justified by reference to the Bible. Had not the Devil, with God's permission, carried Jesus to the pinnacle of the temple in Jerusalem? If he could do this to the son of God how easy a task it must be for him to arrange the transport of a few willing old hags to the meetings where they gathered to do him homage.

Different derivations of the word 'Sabbat' are accepted by different writers. 'S'esbettre'—'to frolic' is one suggested source. Montague Summers traces the word from the Phrygian deity Sabazius who was regarded as the patron of licentiousness and worshipped with 'frantic debaucheries'.

Intercourse with Satan, or with devils, was expected of a witch and details of this were extracted and published with some relish. One writer, at the limit of his warped imagination, equipped the Devil with a long, bifurcated penis so that he could enjoy sex and sodomy simultaneously. Boguet says:

> Since there are some who maintain that the coupling with the Devil exists in the imagination only, it will be well to say something here on the subject. The witches' confessions which I have had make me think there is truth in this matter, for they have all admitted that they have coupled with the Devil and that his semen was very cold. One of them added that she had several times taken in her hand the member of the demon which lay with her and that it was as cold as ice and a good finger's length, but not so thick as that of a man. Nearly all witches affirm that this coupling is by no means pleasurable to them, both because of Satan's ugliness and deformity, and because of the physical pain which it causes them.

Notice the confused accusation here, in the same paragraph, of intercourse with both Satan and demons. Boguet explains the lack of pleasure felt by the witch on these intimate occasions by reminding his readers that the Devil was sometimes in the form of a black man but could also assume the shape of some animal like a dog, a ram or a goat. From all these confessions he concludes: 'I am convinced that there is real and actual copulation between a witch and a demon.'

Incubi and succubi were the particular demons who visited

people in their beds. If the occupant of the bed was a woman, the demon who came to her was called an incubus. The female spirit who attended men to satisfy their lusts was the succubus. The idea of these male and female night visitors long preceded witchcraft. The origins of both can be found in the erotic dreams which any normal young adult has experienced. Their association with witches serves as another illustration of the rag-bag of ideas that the witch-hunters put together, although the actual corporeal existence of these spirits had been decided as proved by theologians as early as the time of Thomas Aquinas in the thirteenth century.

Credulity was stretched to the extent of believing that a woman could conceive a child after a visit from an incubus devil. The writers of the *Malleus* concluded that while no demon could generate life, which was the gift of God alone, it could, in its female form, collect semen from a man and keep it fertile long enough to pass it into a woman (the spirit in the meantime having changed its sex and assumed its male aspect).

An accurate estimate of the number of victims of the witchhunters during their three-hundred-year reign of terror is impossible to form. The true figure must certainly have been in the tens, if not hundreds of thousands; one recent book suggested nine million! Records are patchy, but we know from them that Nicholas Remy, a sixteenth-century French judge, boasted of having burnt nine hundred witches in fourteen years. In Germany another judge was responsible for three hundred burnings in three years. In 1589 in one town in Saxony, in one day, a hundred and thirty-three victims died; and three hundred years before the Nazis obliterated Lidice, two villages near Trier were blotted from the map, whilst in another two only a handful of people were left alive.

The method of executing a condemned witch, like all other aspects of witchcraft, was much debated. Thomas Aquinas, frequently quoted in the *Malleus*, had supported the burning of heretics, and Boguet commented:

Now the usual penalty for witches is that they should be burnt, but there is some doubt as to whether they should be burnt alive or whether they should first be strangled. Both these views are upheld by various authorities.

Amongst the higher-priced items on the grim 'Tariff of Torture' from Cologne, are these:

For strangling and burning ⎫ 4 Thalers and 2 for the wood and
For burning alive ⎭ rope

In parts of the Rhineland, the unhappy centre of so much heresy-hunting, victims were sometimes burnt alive in a hut of dry straw; and at Niesse, in Silesia, forty-two men and girls were roasted in an oven built for the purpose. A sentence of death passed in Lorraine in 1596 reads:

> It is deemed and judged that X be condemned to be burnt alive, that he be bound to a stake expressly erected for the purpose at the appointed place for such executions, so that at least he will feel the flames keenly before being suffocated. His goods to be declared forfeit and confiscate to whom they belong, reasonable expenses for the trial first being deducted.

Children were a special case. Boguet wrote:

> I maintain that not only a child witch who has reached the age of puberty, but even one who has not, should be sentenced to death. Yet I would not in such a case employ the usual penalty for witches but some gentler means, such as hanging.

It is just possible to believe that some of the persecutors of these defenceless victims were sincere—sincere, that is, in believing that they were fighting the Devil and resisting his campaign against the work of the Church and the chances of salvation for its followers. But efforts to excuse them on the grounds of either misplaced sincerity or ignorance must suffer many a setback: for instance, when we think of the irony of extracting from the victim's family the cost of the banquet which traditionally followed the execution, and when we notice that, in those areas where confiscation of property was not allowed, few if any witches were found; and when we think of the hypocrisy of the Ecclesiastical Courts, which did not carry out the sentences themselves but relinquished their prisoners to the secular arm with recommendations to mercy, at the same time making it clear that anyone foolish enough to be merciful would be suspected of favouring heretics and be likely to follow them to the fire.

CHAPTER VII

Conclusions

FROM this examination of the nature of the witchcraft against which even tolerant England had found it necessary to pass harsh laws, the only reasonable conclusion is that not only were such as the Lancashire Witches not witches at all, but that the evil system to which they were supposedly devoted never itself had substance.

However, reverting to a previous warning about the confusion surrounding the word, we must again draw attention to the separate threads of witchcraft running through history, three in the main. The Devil-worshipping witch, imposed on a credulous Europe by a Church which claimed to detect the hand of Satan everywhere; the 'cult witch', follower of an old religion, some of whom still practise; and the 'country witch' with her charms and simples.

If the Lancashire Witches were not Satanists could it be that they were adherents of the Old Religion? It predated Christianity and still survives, so there must have been witches of this type in England right through the seventeenth century. The habits of extreme secrecy which they were forced to develop have persisted to the present day amongst most of them. Others, trusting in an end to all possible fear of persecution are prepared, against the advice of their more cautious brethren, to declare themselves.

However, present-day witches who have read Potts' *Discovery* can find no indication in any of its one hundred and eighty pages that any of the men and women on trial belonged to their small but ancient sect. They point out that none of them, nor indeed any of the thousands of tortured men and women on the continent, ever mentioned the chief deity of the witches, the Mother Goddess, or if any did it was ignored by their tormentors who were determined to prove that witches worshipped Satan. No traceable connection therefore can be found between the Lancashire Witches and those of the present day.

Only if the definition of a witch is extended to cover those who are better called 'wisewomen' or 'wisemen' do they stand a chance of inclusion. A 'wiseman' was mentioned in Isobel Roby's trial. Terms such as 'white witch' and 'cunning man' are also used to describe this sort of person, and a Record Office document from the seventeenth century uses the word 'blesser'. Call them what you will, until quite recent times these men and women played an important role in the life of the countryside and in days when there were few doctors to ease the pains and cure the ills of men and animals they often had, if they successfully applied their skill, a considerable clientele. They were not normally regarded as witches. Rather were they people to whom one could resort to detect a witch or get protection from one. They usually practised their craft as individuals, at the most as a family, and were not suspected of holding regular meetings. In 1845 James Crossley was still able to write:

> He who visits Pendle may yet find that charms are generally resorted to amongst the lower classes . . . that each small hamlet has a peculiar and gifted personage . . . that the wiseman and wisewoman, the white witches of our ancestors, still continue their investigations of truth undisturbed by the rural police or the progress of the schoolmaster.

Although two world wars and the rapid development of transport have largely destroyed the old isolated village life, people of this category, effecting cures by herbs or charms or

125

wishful thinking, but possessed, they consider, of powers which have withered as urban civilisation has spread, are by no means extinct. In their simplest form they are the charmers-away of warts.

Just how many of the Lancashire Witches can be considered as 'wisewomen'? Old Demdike almost certainly. It will be remembered that John Nutter of the Bull Hole, when he had a cow which was sick, requested her to 'mend' it. Perhaps the communion bread she asked her grandson to bring to her was for use in a charm, and at the end of Alizon Device's trial the other witches assured the judge that Demdike, had she lived, would have been able to relieve the pedlar John Law's lameness—although little weight can be attached to this statement, since by that time the witches would be clutching at straws.

Old Chattox too was probably of this type. There is the incident where she dug up the skulls at Newchurch. This must have been a known practice as the Act of 1604 had provided penalties for disturbing graves and stealing their contents. Chattox must have had a use for what she dug up, even if it was merely to impress, or frighten, the ignorant. Perhaps in both her case and Demdike's, with whom she shared the teeth, a little reputed skill in the magic arts made for a better living as a beggar? In another place we read that she was sent for by the wife of John Moore 'to help drink that was forspoken, or bewitched', and the incantation she used on this occasion was quoted at her trial, 'Three biters hast thou bitten. . . .' These incantations, or 'prayers', to be recited when needed, written on paper to be worn in a locket, or even swallowed, were all part of the stock-in-trade of 'wisewomen'. Little Jennet disclosed two, taught to her, she said, by her mother, which gives us cause to think that Elizabeth Device might, not unexpectedly, have followed Old Demdike in this calling. The first 'prayer' revealed by Jennet, and used to get drink, ran: 'Crucifixus hoc fignum vitam Eternam. Amen.' The second, which Jennet was able to recite in court, was for the curing of one bewitched.

Whatever its origin this pathetic piece seems so garbled that it is very doubtful if it had any meaning to its users. As retailed by Potts it ran:

> Vpon Good Friday I will fast while I may
> Until I hear them knell
> Our Lords own Bell,
> Lord in his messe
> With his twelue Apostles good,
> What hath he in his hand
> Ligh in leath wand:
> What hath he in his other hand?
> Heauens doore key,
> Open, open Heauen doore keyes,
> Steck, steck hell doore.
> Let Crizum child
> Goe to it Mother mild,
> What is yonder that casts a light so farrandly,
> Mine owne deare Sonne that's nailed to the Tree.
> He is nailed fore by the heart and hand,
> And holy harne Panne,
> Well is that man,
> That Fryday spell can,
> His childe to learne;
> A Crosse of Blew, and another of Red,
> As good Lord was to the Roode.
> Gabriel laid him downe to sleepe
> Vpon the ground of holy weepe:
> Good Lord came walking by,
> Sleep'st thou wak'st thou Gabriel,
> No Lord I am sted with sticke and stake,
> That I can neither sleepe nor wake:
> Rise vp Gabriel and goe with me,
> The stick nor the stake shall never deere thee.
> Sweet Iesus our Lord, Amen.

If this indeed came from her mother, and was not something Jennet had been carefully coached to recite, it demonstrates the irony of Elizabeth's conviction. Here she was, believing in witchcraft and bewitching, but prepared, like a witch doctor, to use her superstitious knowledge to protect people against witches. (It is not perhaps generally appreciated that the primary function of the African witch doctor is not the working of evil, or the boiling of missionaries in large cauldrons, but the protection of his clients from the evil eye, or the effects of the clay image being used against them.)

If only one in twenty of the wisewoman's charms appeared to produce results both practitioner and client would be convinced that they had real power. Modern generations are just as indulgent to the wisemen and wisewomen of today. Astrologers can misread the stars in the most outrageous way and still retain their reputations on the strength of the odd prophecy that comes off. Racing tipsters, by headlining their successes, yet maintaining a prudent silence about their failures, retain a faithful, if out-of-pocket, band of followers.

If the Demdikes and Chattoxes were 'wisewomen' then the temptation to turn charms to curses for evil ends must have been strong, and the impossible acts of which they were accused may hide many attempted deeds of envy or malice of which they were guilty. Whilst John Nutter, with an ailing cow, sent to Malkin Tower for help, Henry Bulcock, father of a sick child, went there to accuse. If, also, the two old women and possibly Elizabeth had a clientele, they had a reason for their declared rivalry; and it could explain their acquaintance with Alice Nutter who was not of their class, and Katherine Hewitt, who whatever her station in life must have had some motive for travelling from a town several miles away to Malkin Tower. Many today, who would hate to have it known, resort to the naturopath or herbalist, the fortune-teller or medium, when orthodox medicine and religion have proved unsatisfying. In the seventeenth century there was considerable danger in being known to associate with people of this type. King James had written: 'The consulters and entertainers of these craft folk are equally guilty with them that are the practicers.'

In a book in which we have always tried to draw a clear distinction between fact and fiction we must emphasise that these last few paragraphs are speculative. Are we justified in accepting as likely James Device's story of his grandmother asking him to bring her the communion bread, when in the very next sentence he tells us that he was met on the way home by a very aggressive hare, which threatened to pull him to pieces when it found that he had eaten the bread?

In contrast with those parts of Europe in the relentless grip of inquisitors, in England it was always possible for people who opposed the popular delusions of their day to express themselves openly, and one of the first counterblasts of sanity against supposed witchcraft came, when the persecution had barely started, from the pen of one Reginald Scot, a layman with the courage to make his voice heard on a subject usually considered to be the province of lawyers and clergy. Scot was born in 1538 and studied at Oxford before taking up the life of a country gentleman. Many a man whose leisure pastimes have never included a study of witchcraft is unknowingly indebted to him, as his first book, *The Hop Garden* (1574), encouraged and improved the growing of hops, and hence the brewing of beer, in his native Kent.

In 1584, ten years after *The Hop Garden*, came his *Discoverie of Witchcraft*, probably provoked by the trial at Chelmsford in 1582 of the witches of St Osyth. Scot used 'discovery', as Potts did twenty-eight years later, to mean 'uncovering' rather than 'finding'. His opinions, living as he did at the time of the witch trials, are particularly enlightening. Whilst neither he, nor indeed any other writer of his time, flatly denied the existence of witches, he poured scorn on the belief in witches' power and was scathing about the antics of their persecutors. If such a book as his had been brought out on the continent it would probably have led to the arrest of the author, the extraction under torture of a recantation of his views and his eventual burning. Even in England some risk must have attached to the publishing of opinions so contrary to those expressed by the laws then in force.

I

Scot's book is easier to read than most on the subject. In a strongly-worded introduction he speaks of the tyranny and barbarous cruelty which resulted from the absurd inventions and plain knavery of the witch-hunters, and while the *Malleus* had dealt solemnly, and at inordinate length with incubi and succubi, and the supposed power of witches over the privy parts of men, Scot's scornful treatment of these absurd and neurotic fantasies provides some of the few genuinely amusing chapters in what is otherwise a grim tale of man's inhumanity to man or, more usually, woman.

> I must entreat you that are readers, whose chaste ears cannot endure to hear of such abominable lecheries as are gathered out of the books of the witch mongers, to pass over the next eight chapters.

This warning probably ensured, as it would today, that these eight short chapters had the reader's full, if not first, attention. They include these bawdy items, culled by Scot from books on witchcraft and exposed for the ridicule they deserve:

> . . . in the night time an incubus devil came to a young lady's bedside, and made hot love to her; whereat, she being offended, cried out so loud that company came and found him under her bed, but in the likeness of the holy Bishop Sylvanus, which holy man was much defamed thereby!
>
> . . . another young man (who had been deprived of his virile member by a witch) went to her for the restitution thereof. She brought him to a tree and showed him a nest and bad him climb up and take it. And being at the top of the tree he took out a mighty great one, and showed the same to her, asking if he might not have it. 'Nay,' quoth she, 'that is our Parish Priest's toole, take one of the others.'

However, reason, rather than ridicule, was the chief of Scot's methods as he dealt with the less titillating aspects of witchcraft. On the subject of confessions he wrote:

> Note how easily they might be brought to confess that which they never did. They which are commonly accused of witchcraft are the least sufficient of all persons to speak for themselves,

the extremity of their age giving them leave to dote, their poverty to . . . be full of imagination. . . .
The poor old witch is commonly unlearned, unwarned, and unprovided of counsel and friendship . . . void of judgement and discretion. She is daunted by authority, circumvented with guile, compelled by fear, deceived by ignorance and so brought to these absurd confessions. . . .

One sort commonly said to be witches are women which are old, lame, blear-eyed, foul and full of wrinkles. Poor, sullen and superstitious creatures in whose drowsy minds the Devil hath a fine seat. So as whatever mischief is brought to pass they are easily persuaded the same is done by themselves. These wretches are so odious to their neighbours and so feared that few dare offend them or deny them anything they ask—from this they come to think that they can do such things as are beyond the ability of human nature.
They go from door to door for a potful of milk or potage without which they could hardly live. It happens sometimes that their expectations go unanswered as in course of time the witch becomes tedious to her neighbours. So sometimes she curses one, then the other, until, as they all displease her, she curses master, wife, children and cattle.
In time some of her neighbours fall sick, or their cattle die, and they suppose it to be the vengeance of witches. The witch, on the other hand, seeing one in every hundred of her curses take effect, is convinced that she herself has brought this misfortune to pass, and confesses it.
So she, her accusers, and the justices, are all deceived.

How fittingly this describes such as Demdike hobbling home with her begged can of blue milk, willing to use a charm for this neighbour, but cursing that one; and Chattox, stealing a mug of ale from the farmer's wife for whom she was carding wool. Shakespeare's witches were modelled on such as Scot describes; they were essentially poor old women, ragged, skinny and full of vulgar spite. He had nothing to do with the erotic aspects of their nature so much emphasised abroad.

Reginald Scot died in 1599 and it is unfortunate that the principal result of his enlightened and at times humorous outbursts was to provoke an energetic reaction from a source which few dared gainsay, for King James, in the preface of his *Demonology*, stated that one of his motives for writing it had been:

> . . . to resolve the doubting hearts of many against the damnable opinions of one Scot, an Englishman who is not ashamed in public print to deny that there can be such a thing as witchcraft.

When he became king of England, James ordered copies of the *Discoverie of Witches* to be destroyed, yet towards the end of his reign his views had undergone a considerable change, largely because of the frequency with which cases of possession by devils were found to be counterfeits.

In England accusations of witchcraft arose from a variety of circumstances. Sometimes people suffering the ordinary ills of life convinced themselves that some of their neighbours were responsible, and charged them accordingly. At other times individuals or families quarrelled and made spiteful accusations against each other. Both these circumstances were present in the examinations heard by Nowell, but although, as we have seen, a child of nine was easily persuaded to give damning evidence, it was never suggested that Jennet herself, like Grace Sowerbutts of Samlesbury, was in any way the victim of witches or the devils they commanded. This latter situation was the start of many of the most tragic English witch trials—the pretended possession of malicious children who were prepared to say, and demonstrate, that in the presence of certain adults they became subject to uncontrollable fits and convulsions.

An example had some bearing on the Lancashire trials of both 1612 and 1633. In 1597 two children of John Starkie of Cleworth, near Leigh, were amongst seven 'possessed' by demons. This possession was typical of many similar cases but fortunately in this instance the consequence was not the death of some innocent old woman but the hanging of a man called Hartley, a charlatan who had persuaded the Starkies that nothing but his continued presence and entertainment in their house could ward off further visitations. The interest of the case is that Roger Nowell was related, through his mother, to the Starkies, who besides Cleworth had a house at Huntroyd, not far from Read. Also John Starkie, one of the children possessed, was the same who, as a magistrate, listened to and believed Edmund Robinson's mischievous lies in 1633.

In James' reign a number of such similar cases involving children as victims were exposed as completely false and these cases had their effect on his opinions. As he had taken an active personal part in Scottish trials years before, we now find him ordering enquiries, rebuking judges, and himself uncovering the impostures of a young boy at Leicester. This lad's pretended fits had resulted in the execution of nine witches. James, on a timely visit to the town, intervened, and of the six remaining in prison five were released, one unhappily died, and the judges were admonished, rather late in the day, for hanging the others. In the last nine years of James' reign the courts, not surprisingly, became more cautious and only five executions took place.

Eighty years after Reginald Scot's work another book, this time written within sight of Pendle Hill, helped to strengthen the tide by then running strongly in the direction of reason. It was John Webster's *Displaying of Supposed Witchcraft*. Webster was the young curate who, forty years before, had unsuccessfully tried to enquire into the witch-finding activities of the Robinsons of Wheatley Lane. He spent much of his later life near Clitheroe. Like Scot he attacked with vigour the cruelties the witch-belief encouraged, making helpless old women the victims of wicked children, fatuous officials, ignorant neighbours and mobs. Without denying witchcraft he rejected the idea that it was as extensive as was supposed, and he particularly set out to show that whilst witches may have existed and the Devil, on scriptural authority, certainly did, the charges against them of making an actual covenant with Satan, having intercourse with him, allowing him to suck at some part of their body, or having the ability to change their form, were falsely levelled, as all these things were impossibilities. He quoted from Reginald Scot, Thomas Potts and King James. Referring to James he threw doubt on the authorship of *Demonology*, saying: 'There is a little treatise in latin titled 'Deamonologia, fathered upon King James, how truly we shall not dispute for some ascribe it to others.' He was probably referring to another seventeenth-century rationalist, Thomas Ady, who had questioned James' authorship of *Demonology*, suggesting that it had been 'ghost written' by the Bishop of Winchester.

In Webster's book, in pages three centuries old, the modern student will find confirmation of nearly every conclusion at which he is likely to have arrived.

On the sources of the belief and the reasons for its continuance:
Not long after 1300 was the Inquisition set up in Rome and Spain and then did the inquisitors and their adherents draw in from other authors whatsoever might carry any colour of authority or reason, the better to countenance their bloody and unjust proceedings. They drew thousands into the snare of the Inquisition for pretended witchcraft, which they made to be heresy.

On the books of the witch-finders:
A numerous company of authors have written of witchcraft, in sundry ages, of divers countries and in various languages. Yet have they for the most but borrowed from one another, or transcribed what others have written before them.

On confessions:
Although you should find some confidently confessing that they have made a league with the Devil, and that he hath carnal copulation with them, and that he doth suck upon some parts of their bodies . . . or that they fly through the air and raise tempests, yet . . . there never hath been any such witch existent. As there are active witches, whose existence we freely acknowledge, so there are another sort that are under a delusion. They suck in with their mother's milk the gross and erroneous opinions of the vulgar people and confidently believe that they see, do and suffer many strange, odd and wonderful things, which indeed have no existence, only in their depraved fancies.

134

CONCLUSIONS

And yet the confessions of these, though absurd, idle, foolish, false and impossible are taken to be truth, and sufficient ground to condemn the confessors to death.

On attributing to witches the ordinary calamities of life, and on 'possessions' and exorcism:

Many attribute natural diseases and accidents to witches and witchcraft when in truth there is no such matter at all. Sometimes they counterfeit strange fits and diseases, as vomiting of preturnatural and strange things.

The diabolical counterfeiting of possession, the maintaining of the power of casting forth of devils, was not only upheld and maintained by the papists to advance their superstitious causes, but also there were divers nonconformists who, to gain credit and repute, did labour to prove the continuance of real possession by devils and that they had power by fasting and prayer to cast them out.

Webster referred specifically to the possession in the Starkie family:

That discourse concerning possession . . . in Lancashire, in 1594, is of no better grain, but full of untruths, impossibilities, absurdities and contradictions.

It is only fair to mention here that in 1603, following the involvement and eventual exposure of a clergyman in incidents of possession and exorcism which had included the one just referred to, a new canon of the Church of England decreed:

No minister or ministers, without licence and direction of the bishop, shall attempt on any pretext whatsoever to cast out any devils under pain of the imputation of imposture and deposition from the ministry.

On witch-finders and their handling of suspects, of which he had personal experience, Webster wrote:

Divers innocent persons lost their lives, and these wicked rogues wanted no greater persons (even in the ministry) to encourage them and authorise them. The like in my time happened here in Lancashire, where both men and women were accused of supposed witchcraft, and were so unchristianly and inhumanly handled as to be stripped stark naked and laid

135

upon tables and beds to be searched (nay even in their most privy parts) for these supposed witch marks.

He was referring here to the activities of unofficial witch-finders and 'prickers', although searching, in a less barbarous way we would hope, was undertaken by magistrates, as we read in the case of Elizabeth Device at Read. It was also done in prison. Years after the Lancashire Witches had gone from the scene, in what must have been one of the last witch trials at Lancaster, worthy women were still being called upon to examine their unfortunate sisters in the cells. An account from Webster's time says:

> One Katherine Walkden of Atherton was committed to Lancaster as a witch. She was examined by a jury of matrons who discovered a private teat, and upon this and other evidence was convicted.

Webster understandably, as we know him to have held office in the Church, wrote at length on the mistaken connection between the scriptures and the witchcraft of the inquisitors. James I had sustained his case against the witches by frequent biblical quotations. Webster challenged the contention that as witch-craft was mentioned in the Bible it was wrong, in fact heretical, not to believe in it.

> There is not one word in scripture that signifies a witch in the sense that is vulgarly intended. When the Inquisitors, the popish doctors and writers had found the sweetness and benefit of the confiscated goods of those that they had caused to be accused and condemned for witches, words which in the true sense did but signify a secret poisoner were wrested to signify a witch that made a visible and corporeal league with the Devil.

Thus the witch of Endor would be better described as a necromancer or medium, and in Exodus 'Thou shalt not suffer a witch to live', whilst 'witch' was used in the Authorised Version (authorised, be it remembered, by James I) most others, including the Revised and Moffat translations, replace it by 'sorceress'.

136

Webster's refutation of biblical authority can be effectively summarised in two brief quotations from other sources. The Thomas Ady who had doubted James' authorship wrote a book aptly titled *A Candle in the Dark*. In this he asked:

> Where is it written in the Bible that a witch is a murderer, can afflict with disease or infirmity, hurt corn or cattle or fly through the air?
> Where is it written that witches have imps sucking at their bodies or that the Devil sets private marks on them? Where do we hear of an incubus or succubus?

Nearer our own times, Sir Walter Scott, in *Letters on Demonology and Witchcraft*, emphatically stated:

> There is not a word in scripture authorising us to believe that a system existed in any respect similar to that against which the law books of so many European nations have decreed punishment. Witchcraft was part of that mass of errors which appeared among the members of the Christian Church when their religion became gradually corrupted by the devices of men.

Those who know only of his novels may be surprised at his concern with the subject of witches. Doubtless his early acquaintance with Potts stirred his interest, although Scottish history is full enough of them.

Finally, John Webster had first-hand knowledge of the ways of 'wisewomen' and of the superstitious beliefs of the clients they served, and in writing of them he provides us with some new and interesting names for the species.

> We ourselves have practised the art of medicine in the north of England, where ignorance, popery and superstition abound, and where the common people, if they chance to have any sort of epilepsy, palsy, convulsion or the like do persuade themselves that they are bewitched. If you should by plain reason show them that they are deceived they account you a physician of small value. But if you indulge their fancy, or hang any insignificant thing round their necks, assuring them that it is the most efficacious and powerful charm, you may settle their imagina-

tions, then give them what is proper to eradicate the disease. And so you may cure them, as we have done in great numbers. For it is here in the North country, where our figure flingers and pretended conjurers, piss prophets and water witches, that if they hit once it is cried up and told everywhere, but if they err an hundred times, it is soon buried in silence and oblivion. We call them wisemen or wisewomen, without regard to the ways or means by which they find stolen goods, or help men or animals thought to be bewitched.

Very gradually the voices of reason which had been raised against the persecution began to prevail and the belief in witches faded. Christian European thought was coaxed back from the influence of the *Malleus Maleficarum* to the saner sentiments of the 'Canon Episcopi'. One has only to reflect on how considerably attitudes to such things as capital punishment, mental illness, abortion or illegitimacy have changed in our own times to realise that alterations in the public mood have many causes, not always easy to define. One thing is certain, the cruel and fanatical campaigns of the witch-hunters were not responsible for the eventful disappearance of their victims and on the continent a significant move which immediately dampened their ardour was the forbidding, in 1630, by the Holy Roman Emperor of the appropriation of property. The laws which give expression to changes are sometimes ahead of public opinion, sometimes behind it. At the start of the witch persecution ordinary people, for whom magic and sorcery were part of life, had nevertheless needed converting by the propaganda of the day: books, sermons, public confessions. Eventually, when educated and official ideas changed, there were many instances of the common people, still afraid of witches, taking the law into their own hands, swimming, maltreating and occasionally killing people suspected of doing harm to their neighbours by employing a witch's methods. But it was as workers of evil magic that they were feared, not as members of some devil-worshipping coven.

During the years of persecution, in contrast to the hysterical slaughter abroad, reasonable estimates of the numbers of those hanged, in England, or burnt in Scotland, would be one thousand and four thousand respectively. Scotland, moderate in numbers compared with Germany, had ranked second to none in the barbarous use of torture. Cases in Ireland were so few as to be insignificant. England had started later than most countries, never shown excessive zeal and in consequence came to its senses sooner. In 1684, at Exeter, three 'very old, decrepit and impotent women', Susannah Edwards, Mary Trembles and Temperence Lloyd, who had all confessed to seeing the Devil and to harbouring familiars, were hanged. Some books give this as the last judicial hanging of witches in England, but in 1686, again in Exeter, Alice Molland too was hanged as a witch, the last of the few hundred men and women to suffer death under the various laws which had been in force since 1542. In 1712 Jane Wenham of Hertford was tried, pronounced guilty, but reprieved, in the last of the witch trials. In 1717 Jane Clark of Great Wigton was indicted at Leicester for witchcraft, but the charge was not proceeded with.

In 1736 came the last of the Witchcraft Acts. But whereas the previous statutes, under Henry VIII in 1542, Elizabeth in 1563 and James in 1604, had been concerned with punishing witches, this one gave expression to the new and enlightened attitude now prevailing. It repealed the one of 1604 which had for long been in disuse, and it prescriped punishments, not for witches, but for any who brought accusations of witchcraft. The last paragraph of the new Act also made it an offence 'to pretend to exercise or use any kind of witchcraft, sorcery, enchantment, or conjuration, or undertake to tell fortunes . . . or discover where . . . any [stolen or lost] goods or chattels . . . may be found'. Although fortune-telling has been openly tolerated, it was under this Act that many unfortunate mediums were prosecuted, until in 1951 the Witchcraft Act of George II was replaced by the Fraudulent Mediums Act. There was some opposition to the more enlightened laws. John Wesley was one of the reactionaries. In his journal, 20 May 1768, following a diatribe against freethinkers, he states:

It is true that the English in general, and indeed most of the men of learning in Europe, have given up all accounts of witchcraft and apparitions, as mere old wives' fables. I am sorry for this; and I willingly take this opportunity of entering my solemn protest against this violent compliment which so many that believe the Bible pay to those who do not believe it.

And so, from 24 June 1736, the dwindling belief in witchcraft was officially condemned. It had been fifty-two years since the last execution in England and twenty-four since the last trial. Along with the burning of heretics and the flogging of harlots the hanging of witches had mercifully come to an end.

CHAPTER VIII

Sources and Traces

THE original documents which were available to Thomas Potts cannot now be traced. He says they were 'with the clerke of the Crown at Lancaster'. Unfortunately the Clerk of the Crown's records for the Palatinate of Lancaster which would otherwise have been in the Public Record Office in London have not survived for the year 1612. Also there is no Assize Roll for that date. Copies of many of these Assize Rolls are to be found in the Farrer collection of documents in the Manchester Central Library but again there are none for 1612. In the Lancashire Record Office at Preston are many papers of preliminary hearings taken before Justices of the Peace, but there is a gap in these from about 1606 to 1624. For other years about thirty are listed in the catalogue under 'witchcraft'. They are all handwritten on strong paper and formally headed in the fashion faithfully copied by Potts from Roger Nowell. The writing is invariably cramped and in a style very different from that of today, but one searches in vain for the names of Southern, Whittle, Nutter or Nowell!

Outside the pages of Potts only one certain reference to any of the witches of 1612 can be found. This is in the 'House and Farm Accounts of the Shuttleworths of Gawthorpe' for the printing of which the Chetham Society was also responsible. An item for July 1612 is: 'the constable of Padiham, to the carriage of Pearson, his wife to Lancaster,—3/10—.' Constables' expenses were met either by selling the goods of offenders or by levying a tax on the townsfolk. This was the Shuttleworths' share when Margaret Pearson was sent for trial at the instigation of Nicholas Bannister. The accounts were kept by a steward, and his entry for a date in August that year, just after the mention of 'Pearson's wife', suggests that his master, Sir Richard Shuttleworth, who was a young man of about twenty-five at the time, himself went to the Assizes. The entry reads: 'to my Mr. before he went towardes Lancaster, xl S., given to my Mr. to put in his pocket, xx S.'

Two other items of indirect interest. One of them is on 24 April 1613, and records the payment of sixpence '. . . towards the bringing up of Besse Chattocks cloths'. Bessie is mentioned only once in Potts: '. . . a daughter of Anne Chattox called Elizabeth having been at the house of Iohn Nutter of the Bull-hole to begge a dish full of milke', although it could have been she who was seen by Alizon Device wearing some of the clothes stolen from Malkin Tower. Although her mother and sister were hanged as witches, she herself does not appear to have been accused, and what she was doing at Lancaster, presumably in the prison, is a mystery. Just one more item in the accounts concerns witches—a recurring phenomenon it seems in those parts. '26 May. 1620 to the constable of Padiham, towards the watching of the supposed witches xxij d.' Who these were, or what their ultimate fate was, is not known.

In *The Farington Papers*, again a Chetham Society publication, there is mention of Thomas Covell. Although in his seventies he was still the gaoler at Lancaster when William Farington was sheriff in 1636. These papers give some fascinating side-lights on the preparations for the Assizes in the seventeenth century. Also among the papers is a short list, dated August 1636, of 'Witches remaining in his Majesty's Gaol'. It includes Marie Spencer, Jennet Hargreaves, Frances Dickinson and Jennet Device, four of the women tried in 1633; one wonders, after the conclusions reached by the king's enquiry, what they were doing still in the cells?

Another Chetham Society book with some slight connection

with the Lancashire Witches is the journal of Nicholas Assheton of Downham, which has survived for the years 1617–18. Nicholas' elder brother Richard, who died about 1597, had been, according to Chattox, one of Demdike's earlier victims. Particularly interesting is the vivid account which the diary gives of the life of the gentry of those parts and those days. In the short space of time covered, Nicholas recorded sixteen fox-hunts, ten stag-hunts, and another fifteen days spent hunting otter, hare, buck and badger, grouse-shooting, hawking, or fishing in the Ribble. There are nineteen confessions of drunkenness, ranging from merely 'merrie' to 'sicke with drinke'. The journal also makes obvious the intermarrying of families and frequent meeting of the gentry, particularly at Assizes and Quarter Sessions. Shuttleworth, Holden, Gerard, Starkie, Lister and Bannister find frequent mention. Roger Nowell of Read is named only once, and although another entry records a night spent making merry and playing shuffleboard with Nowell's son, one gains the impression that the two families were not on very intimate terms. Assheton gives a most interesting account of the visit of King James I to Lancashire, and particularly to Hoghton Tower. On this occasion Nicholas was content to attend Sir Richard Hoghton and wear his livery, although as he explains, lest we should think him too servile, 'rather from his grace and reputation, showing his neighbour's love, than any exacting of mean service'.

It is clear that Harrison Ainsworth was acquainted with this journal and the hunting, the feasting, the masquing, which attended this royal visit to Lancashire were too much for him to miss. He put up no sort of resistance to temptation, and, ignoring the five-year gap between the king's arrival at Hoghton in 1617 and the execution of the witches at Lancaster in 1612, he unashamedly infiltrated a few of them into the royal presence, and set the last part of his book in the splendid surroundings of Hoghton Tower. Nicholas he enlisted as one of the characters in his book, but in contrast to his license with dates the per-

143

sonality he attributed to him was perfectly justified. He says 'Nicholas Assheton of Downham, might be considered a type of the Lancashire squire of his day, although constant in attendance at church and lecture, he put no sort of restraint upon himself, but mixed up fox hunting, shooting . . . foot racing, horse racing, and in fact, every other kind of country diversion, not forgetting tippling, carding and dicing, with daily devotion and psalm-singing in the oddest way imaginable.'

By the time James I came to Hoghton, his opinions on witchcraft had, as described in the previous chapter, undergone a change, if he had not in fact lost interest in the subject. His early zeal and abnormal interest in them are explained in an old anonymous pamphlet, *Newes from Scotland, Declaring the Damnable Life and Death of Dr Fian* (1591). James became king of Scotland, the sixth of that name, in 1567. In 1589 he chose Anne, younger daughter of King Frederick of Denmark, as his bride, and was married to her by proxy. She set sail for Scotland but was driven back by storms which forced her to land and stay in Norway. So James embarked on one of the few venturesome undertakings of his life, and went to fetch her. They were married in Oslo, by a minister from the Scottish Kirk who had been taken over for the purpose, and James spent the rest of the winter in Copenhagen with his pretty and intelligent young wife 'making good cheer and drinking stoutly till the spring time'. When he returned from Denmark, he was persuaded that the storms which had prevented Anne's crossing the previous year, and the ones he had endured on his own journeys, had been contrived by a group of witches operating in East Lothian. Members of this unfortunate group were apprehended and some of them cruelly tortured. The whole sad train of events as revealed by this old document started when one David Seaton, Deputy Bailiff of the town of Trenant, became suspicious of the regular absence from his house of a servant girl— Geillis Duncan. She refused to explain herself, so her master resorted to harsh treatment. Her fingers were crushed and her head was bound with a rope and viciously 'thrown'—wrenched about. She then disclosed that her going out every other night was for the purpose of visiting and healing people with sickness or infirmity, and it transpired that her power to do this was considered almost miraculous. She had been wise to be secretive about herself, for Seaton immediately suspected that such reputed miracles could only be the work of the Devil, and after further brutality he got Geillis to admit to this, and say that she did her work by witchcraft in concert with others. Two she named as Agnes Sampson and Dr John Fian.

Agnes Sampson, described as a woman 'of rank above the vulgar', was taken to Holyrood House and questioned before the king and sundry nobles. She denied all acquaintance with witchcraft until she had been subjected to 'such torture as hath been lately provided for witches'. Besides being tortured she had all the hair shaved from her body so that better search could be made for the Devil's mark, which was eventually located 'on her privities'. Not unnaturally Agnes broke down under this outrageous and humiliating treatment. She gave her tormentors a detailed description of a meeting of over two hundred witches at which the plot against the king had been hatched. They had, she said, concluded a merry night of drinking by dancing a reel in North Berwick Kirk, having first sailed there in sieves. The Devil had been in attendance and had demanded his usual token of submission—a kiss on the buttocks. These he obligingly exposed as he lay over the pulpit. The king, who 'took great delight to be present at their examinations', believed all these fantasies. The other suspect, Dr Fian, schoolmaster of Trenant, had his nails torn off with pincers and pins driven into the exposed raw flesh. His knees were crushed in a vice and his fingerbones splintered. He eventually gave way and confessed to anything that was suggested to him. But Fian was a brave man. He recovered sufficiently to retract his first confession and thenceforward withstood all further agonies until he was burnt on Castle Hill at Edinburgh in January 1591.

K

Parish registers are a happy hunting ground for historians, but here again as concerns the Lancashire Witches, entries are uncertain or indirect. In those for Padiham, dated 9 August 1581, is the record of a wedding between Edward Pearson and Margaret Bowker. This bride of yesteryear might be the woman who was made to suffer, in her home town as well as in three others, the indignities of the pillory for the killing of Dodgson's mare. The Dodgsons themselves are well represented in this particular register, the entries under that name being spelt in fifteen different ways.

In the Newchurch registers for 1592 are recorded the baptism and death of the infant 'Jacobus Redferne', who could have been a son of Anne's. The entry is at any rate a pointer to the respectability of some part of the Redfearn family since the baptism of infants was not always sought by the peasantry. In the parish registers of Colne an Alice Gray is shown as being buried on 29 April 1613—possibly the onetime companion of Katherine Hewitt. Every register in this area contains many entries under 'Nutter', but the family and its widespread branches is difficult to sort out. Although landowners they were of a lower social class than the Nowells of Read, or the Asshetons of Downham. None of them bore arms or attended the heralds who made periodic visits to the county for the purpose of examining and registering the family pedigrees (there was one such visit in 1613). Although most of those who nowadays bear the name allege descent from Alice Nutter of Roughlee, apart from the certain fact that she had a son, Myles, her descendants are not traceable. There must have been others in her family because it is mentioned that 'her own children' could never get her to confess.

Very few people have read *The Wonderful Discovery of Witches*, but many are familiar with the two novels, *The Lancashire Witches*, and *Mist over Pendle*. It is probably from these that many local people believe in a family feud between the Nowells and the Nutters, the result of some boundary dispute. Several other books mention this tradition, but one has copied the other and there is no reliable confirmation, nor anything to show that Roger Nowell had any motive for seeking the downfall of Mistress Nutter. She will probably always remain an asset to novelists but an enigma for the rest of us. It must always be borne in mind that Ainsworth was a great romancer. Before he came upon the story of Lancashire witchcraft he had romanticised Dick Turpin, and in a later work, *Crichton*, he elevated another rascal, Jack Sheppard, to the rank of hero. (Sheppard was a notorious escaper from gaols and one of the cells which housed him can be seen, rebuilt, in Madame Tussaud's in London.) Not surprisingly, Ainsworth used his imaginative talents in dealing with witches. As we have seen with the royal visit to Hoghton Tower he transposed events without conscience if it suited his plot. He rewarded Thomas Potts, to whom indeed we are all much indebted, with an important but quite unjustified role in *The Lancashire Witches*. Potts is unlikely in real life to have strayed from the circuit and come any nearer to Pendle Forest than the road from Lancaster to London, but in the novel he is used by the author for the ageless theme of the discomforting of the city dweller by rustics, and is made to venture into Pendle Forest to suffer humiliation at the hands of the local populace.

Ainsworth entirely invented his own Alizon, endowing her with extreme beauty, natural grace and a sweet voice. He happily transformed this delinquent beggar maid into a beauty who could mix on easy terms with kings and nobles, finally revealing that she was in fact not of the Demdike brood, but the daughter of Alice Nutter. Alizon's lot in reality must have been sadly different. The Court Rolls of Gisburn where Jennet Preston lived give evidence of the unpopularity of those who chose, or were compelled by circumstances, to live as beggars. Since the Poor Law Acts had made each parish responsible for the destitutes within its bounds, and had authorised a compulsory levy for their support, any person remaining in a parish for more than a month could be considered the responsibility of that

147

parish, and would have to be maintained; it was therefore in everybody's interests to drive him on. At Gisburn it was decreed that anyone who should harbour a beggar 'above two or three nights' should be liable to a fine of ten shillings.

If documents directly connected with the Lancashire Witches are hard to find there is no dearth of material on witchcraft in general. Rossell Hope Robbins' *Encyclopedia of Witchcraft and Demonology* lists 1,140 items in what can still be called a select bibliography—a daunting collection. Even with guidance there are pitfalls. In looking for authorities students are usually referred to one or other of the late Dr Margaret Murray's books. Far from concluding that witchcraft in the sixteenth and seventeenth centuries was largely an invention of the Church, Dr Murray's books postulate an extensive underground organisation of witches, claiming at one time in our history thousands of adherents from all classes of society—not excluding royalty. These, she maintains, had their own priests and ceremonies and met regularly, just as King James had described, to pay homage to the Devil. Beginners naturally hesitate to challenge Dr Murray's conclusions, even when they find her quoting the parts of confessions which support her theories and ignoring the parts which do not. She is always over-anxious to have her witches in tidy covens of thirteen, and in her *Witch Cult in Western Europe* her most obvious error concerning the Lancashire Witches is to include Isobel Roby in her number for the Pendle Area. This is an unjustifiable error, overlooking as it does the fact that Isobel lived thirty-five miles from Pendle and just happened to be at the same Assizes. It is a relief that Dr Murray's ideas on this subject, about which she has written so extensively, are now generally considered to be extravagant and speculative.

Outside the pages of books, traces of the Lancashire Witches in their home county and district are few, mostly indirect and in one important case doubtful. Pendle has so far been spared the establishment of any witchcraft museum. There are several of these in various parts of our islands; some are good, but nothing better exemplifies the confusion surrounding the word 'witch' than the haphazard collections of charms, cauldrons and instruments of torture found in others.

The boundaries of Pendle Forest are shown on the map. They have little significance these days, the whole area now being administered as part of Burnley Rural District. A dominant feature to the west is Pendle Hill. This is just over eighteen hundred feet high and no reasoning will ever convince the children of the area that the old habit of putting a stone on the summit cairn was not an attempt by devoted locals to raise the height to two thousand feet: youngsters hold fast to the belief that this would transform Pendle Hill into Pendle Mountain. Pen meant hill in Celtic times (Penyghent is not many miles away); this meaning was lost, and the hill came to be called Penhull, or Penhill, later changed to Pendle. Nowadays, making trebly certain, it bears the name Pendle Hill. Detachment from the main range of the Pennines makes it more prominent than its modest height deserves, and it is popular with ramblers, being so near the industrial towns of North East Lancashire; on Good Fridays, if the weather is fine, it is positively infested by walkers—an annual invasion not linked with the famous conclave on that day in 1612! Around midsummer, on fine Saturday nights, hundreds of people will climb to the top, there to wait hopefully for the often dramatic sunrises. The view from the summit can be magnificent. In conditions of exceptional clarity the Welsh Hills, Blackpool Tower, the Irish Sea, and the hills of the Lake District, are all plainly visible, but the only reported case of York Minster being seen from Pendle is unfortunately fictional—from the first pages of Harrison Ainsworth's *Lancashire Witches*. The picture of a coven of hags astride their broomsticks sweeping silently across the bleak expanse of Pendle is an intriguing one. It is with some sadness that we must point out that not once within the covers of Thomas Potts' book was Pendle Hill mentioned. And not once was there any reference to a broomstick.

The elevated part of the Forest around Pendle Hill, as one would expect, is of little use except as grazing for sheep, and as a gathering ground for water. On the valley slopes, particularly the south-facing ones, the land is relatively good, although nowhere is it as fertile as in the rich alluvial plain of the Ribble, a few miles to the north. The area has an abundant supply of soft, lime-free water, which led to the establishment in the nineteenth century of four cotton mills on this stretch of Pendle Water. Round two of these, at Roughlee and Barley, grew the present villages. One of the mills was working until 1967 and traces of the other three can be found.

Although originally this 'forest' was one of the areas set aside by the De Lacys, Norman lords of Clitheroe, for hunting and the rearing of deer, as early as the thirteenth century 'vaccaries' or cow-farms had been established within its bounds and the names they bore, such as Roughlee Booth, or Goldshaw Booth, survive to the present day as divisions of the Forest. It is probably more thickly wooded now than it ever was, but this is because of tree-planting by Nelson Corporation in relatively recent times, and does not excuse one authority on witchcraft for writing that Demdike lived in the middle of a wood in Lancashire. Potts described the area as a 'vast' place, fit for one of Demdike's profession, using 'vast' in the old sense of empty or unproductive—waste, in fact. Yet a recent survey of seventeenth-century wills and inventories, 'The Forest of Pendle in the Seventeenth Century', by Mary Brigg (*Transactions of the Historic Society of Lancashire & Cheshire*, Vol 113), gives a very different picture. It seems to have been a prosperous area, and by this time all the land was divided into farms; the wolves which strangled the cows, and the wild boars hunted in earlier days, had long since been killed off. All the farms were mixed, the proportion of land devoted to crops and stock depending on the situation, and on the fertility of the soil. Some of the smaller ones were run entirely by the family, and income was supplemented by the spinning and weaving of wool. Oxen ploughed; horses were used to pull carts of coal from Burnley or sledges of peat from the hills, to carry pack-saddles, or for riding. In contrast to the present day much of the land grew corn, mostly oats, often on land today considered marginal and worthy of a subsidy. Some wheat and barley were grown, the latter supplying the Forest's fifteen or so ale-houses. Nowadays, in the evening when the shadows are long, or in winter after a scattering of snow, many fields still reveal the marks of former cultivation, the neat division into strips becoming evident. This had nothing to do with the manorial system so beloved of the writers of school history books. The method of ploughing centuries ago corrugated the land; and fields which have not grown a crop other than grass for many years still display the marks of past usage.

In 1608, James I, short of money, was encouraged by the crown lawyers to assert a claim over the farms. Resulting from this the copy-holders were obliged to part with a sum equal to twelve years' rent to have their right to the land confirmed by Parliament. One of the unavailing arguments which the 'forest' dwellers put forward in resisting the royal demands was mention of the hardship they had in finding material for their houses, 'having no timber there, nor within many miles thereof'. To compensate for this levy they had been fortunate in other ways. In a long period of inflation their rents had remained unrealistically low, and the pattern for the years which have concerned us is of a hard-working population living in the scattered farms, which were well furnished and so well built that many of them survive to this day.

Within Pendle Forest the most notable and certain survival from the days of the witches is Roughlee Hall where Alice Nutter lived. What was once a fine dwelling for one family is now divided into five cottages, and one at least of the present occupants is so wearied of callers that he has a printed card

151

containing a concise history of the house, which is silently handed to enquirers; and the place has had to be declared 'out of bounds' for the children from Whitehough Camp School, who are otherwise encouraged to delve deep into anything of local interest. The house was built in 1536 and apart from television aerials, and the fact that the windows at the west end have been de-mullioned and altered, it must now look very much as it did in the early seventeenth century. Advocates for the preservation of historic buildings should not grumble at the few alterations: old photographs show that not so many years ago it was ruinous, compared with its well-kept condition today.

Not far from Roughlee Hall, on the banks of the Pendle Water, James Crossley described finding in 1845 'the foundations of an ancient mill . . . the millstones still unremoved . . . doubtless the mill of Richard Baldwin the miller'. Time, and the violence of this stream, when it has to find room in its narrow course for the torrents of water which occasionally drench Pendle, have taken away all trace of Baldwin's mill, although there is no reason to doubt the place where it stood. A few miles south from Roughlee is the house where the other Nutters of the story lived—old Robert, Christopher, young Robert. Greenhead is still occupied and is a fine old house. Some of the original glass is in a few of the windows and seeing it makes us realise that our seventeenth-century forbears, whatever their wealth, had to be content with a dim and distorted view of the outside world.

Chattox and the Redfearns lived on land belonging to these Nutters. It was here 'in their own garden', she said, that Demdike found them fashioning clay 'pictures'. By the side of a stream not far from Greenhead, hidden in the long grass, is the base of a building. Between it and the water is a bank of malleable clay and it is easy to picture Demdike, can of milk in hand, surprising Chattox and her daughter at their modelling. Enquiries from the present owner of the land about the old building were for once fruitful—unfortunately! His father had told him how, many years ago, one of the farm hands, anxious perhaps for a bit of independence, had been given permission to keep hens in a hut by the stream. The hoped-for ruins of a seventeenth-century witch's cottage must unhappily be accepted as the foundations of a nineteenth-century hen hut.

One of the unsolved puzzles surrounding the Pendle Witches is the exact site of Malkin Tower, where Old Demdike lived, and with her apparently the whole Device family. Little Jennet referred to it as 'her grandmother's house'. Her brother James called it his mother's, then clarified the position a bit later by saying that it was his grandmother's but now his mother's. The word, frequently spelt 'Mawkin', is pronounced to rhyme with 'talking' without the final 'g'. It was derived from Mary, Maud or Matilda and was formerly a personal name typical of women of the lower classes; by the sixteenth century it had come to

Malkin Tower Farm. The henhut stands on the possible site of Demdike's home. Blacko Tower can be seen in the distance

mean a slut, a drab, or a scarecrow, and occurs in this sense in Shakespeare's *Coriolanus*—'the kitchen malkin pins her richest lockram round her reechy neck'. It was used as a term of abuse or contempt but is now obsolete except in dialect where it is certainly still current in parts of Lancashire. For example, to speak of someone 'malkin into the house' would be to describe a slovenly, slouching entry; and to call a person a 'malk' is to imply sloppiness. It is rarely heard and seems to survive only in some of the remoter country parts. It was also a word used for a cat, or hare. This is confusing where witches are concerned, as the former animal was a popular guise for a witch's familiar, and Malkin, or some variation of it, was often used for his name. 'I come Graymalkin,' cries the first witch in Macbeth! Whether the name derived from the inhabitants or not it is certain that Malkin Tower was the abode of as fine a family of slatterns as any to be found in the county. A theory that the name was a contraction of 'malt kiln' seems to be supported by Alizon's mention of the Chattoxes breaking into their 'firehouse'. However, 'firehouse' was simply a technical term for any dwelling with a hearth.

There is a farm near Blacko called Malkin Tower Farm, and marked thus on the current Ordnance Survey maps. Some older maps say simply 'Malkin'. Within the boundaries of Pendle Forest, although only just, it is near the old road to Gisburn where one of the witches lived, and not very far from Colne, where Alizon went a-begging, and from whence two other women came to the Good Friday meeting. Round the back of the present farm house is the ruin of an older building. One wall, with some mortar holding to the stones, is still upright, and has been incorporated into the field wall, although it is higher and stands out quite plainly. Near to this wall, until recently, was a flagged floor. This site was accepted by Crossley, and many local people have been brought up to believe that it is the location of Demdike's dwelling, to the extent that the farmer admits to getting tired, on summer weekends, of 'show-

154

ing people round the back' as he puts it. The deeds of the farm unfortunately go back only to 1803, about which time it was sold off from a larger estate. Almost certainly the Devices never owned it; they were probably tenants of a labourer's cottage.

An alternative site, not far from the village of Newchurch in Pendle, was suggested by a Dr Laycock of Sabden who many years ago himself wrote and lectured on the Lancashire Witches. In a survey of 1828, made for Teesdale's Map of Lancashire, three fields belonging to Saddler's Farm were reportedly called Malkin Fields. The name seems to have gone out of use, but in a corner of one of the likely fields there has obviously been an old building. When this field was last ploughed this corner had to be left, because the big stones just under the surface were damaging the plough. Although the field boundary is otherwise hedged or fenced, just here is a wall, as though stones were available and had been put to use. Moss End and Bull Hole Farms, both mentioned in the trials, are within yards; and Demdike's son, Christopher Howgate, lived not far away. Demdike confessed to first meeting Tibb near here: 'neere vnto a Stonepit in Gouldshey . . . a Spirit or Deuill in the shape of a Boy, who bade her stay, saying to her, that if she would giue him her Soule, she should haue anything that she would request.' Goldshaw is the name for this part of Pendle Forest near Newchurch. And lastly, James Device, the night before the Good Friday meeting, carried or drove a stolen wether, belonging to a Barley farmer, to his grandmother's house where he killed it. The distance from Barley to the Malkin Tower at Blacko is considerable, but from Saddler's Farm Barley is just over the hill. (There is of course the possibility that the sheep, although the property of a man from Barley, might have been grazing many miles from there.) The voluminous deeds of Saddler's Farm go back to the seventeenth century, but although they include maps on which field names are shown there is no trace of the Malkin fields known to Dr Laycock. The nearest they come is to mention a Kiln Yard, which is hardly the same thing.

It is one of the mysteries of this story that the certain situation of the witches' cottage has been forgotten. As three of its inhabitants were declared to be agents of the Devil and were hanged, it is hardly likely that anyone would wish to live in it when they had gone, and it might have been pulled to pieces deliberately by neighbours, either to destroy its melancholy associations, or simply for the re-use of the stone. It was most likely a simple sort of dwelling—a far cry from the near-fortress of Ainsworth's novel.

A prominent landmark of today, which looks like the sort of place Ainsworth described, is Blacko Tower—less than a mile from Malkin Tower Farm. It is circular, rather ugly, and built on a hill top, right on the Lancashire–Yorkshire border, which here is also the boundary of Pendle Forest. But it is not very old. It was built by one Jonathan Stansfield, a shopkeeper of Barrowford, and erected for no explicable reason about 1891, by a man who after a frugal life could evidently think of nothing better to do with his money. People nowadays call it 'Jonathan's Folly'. About 1950 when it was getting so dangerous that it would have had to be pulled down, it was repaired by a group

Blacko Tower, a landmark for miles around. This is very near to Malkin Tower but has itself no connection with witches

of local volunteers, mostly Scouts, who deserve the gratitude of thousands who live within sight of it. Also, in the process of repairing this Victorian folly they uncovered a piece of much older history: a beautiful bronze axe-head was found in the grass and helped to confirm a doubtful part of a known trade route which had crossed England in the Bronze Age from the Ribble to the Humber. But Blacko Tower has no connection with witches, despite the fact that from 1891, the date it was built, the deeds of Malkin Tower Farm begin to refer to 'Malkin Tower, otherwise Blacko Tower'—a careless error, which once made has been copied since.

In 1529 a church was built in Goldshaw for the convenience of the inhabitants of the four booths of Barley with Wheatley, Roughlee, Old Laund and Goldshaw. In a rather dark corner of the present church is a pew set aside for the use of churchwardens. There are four seats, and over each is still painted the name of the booth to whose warden it was assigned. The church was consecrated in 1544 and dedicated to St Mary. It became known as the Newchurch in Pendle and has given its name to the village which now surrounds it. Little of the original building remains, both nave and tower having been rebuilt, but it is interesting as all old country churches are. Painted on the outside of the tower is what appears to be an eye. Its origin and purpose are mysteries, but it has become known locally as the 'eye of God' and is fancied to give added protection to the worshippers within from the evil which once abounded without.

If an obvious stranger visits the church he will no doubt be shown the 'witch's grave' near the porch. Its manifest age, a skull and crossbones and the name of Nutter on the gravestone have misled many people into believing that this is where Alice Nutter was buried. Although the year on this particular stone is no longer legible, it is known that the earliest date on any stone in the churchyard was 1651. The skull and crossbones was not infrequently used as a symbol of death and does not

157

The Newchurch in Pendle was consecrated in 1544 and gave its name to the village which now surrounds it. The oval stone on the tower is known as 'the eye of God'

in any way connect the occupant of the grave with witchcraft. In any case witches' bodies were customarily cut down and burnt after hanging and not buried in consecrated ground. However, if the graveyard has none to offer, witches galore still abound for visitors to Newchurch and the district. Made from pipe-cleaners, cork and scraps of material, they hang in their dozens in a shop in the village street and sit astride their tiny brooms in practically every bar in every pub for miles around.

As might be expected, links with the well-to-do families, from whose ranks the magistrates were naturally drawn, are easier to find. In Whalley Church can be seen the pew of the Nowells, bearing their coat of arms. It was put in in 1534, and enlarged in 1610, the year Roger Nowell was Sheriff of Lancaster. In this year there was a dispute with the Asshetons about the use of the pew. It was serious enough to be referred to the Bishop of Chester and taken to the Chancery Court at Lancaster, and it may explain the apparent lack of intimacy between the two families, which was suggested by Nicholas Assheton's Journal. Also in the church at Whalley is a fine window emblazoned with twelve coats of arms including, besides those of Nowell, those of Assheton, Bannister, Holden, Starkie and Towneley, all mentioned in this narrative.

Read Hall, where the Nowells lived for many generations, finally passed out of the family's hands in 1772. It was then sold by Court Order to pay the debts of Alexander Nowell, whose income had been insufficient to support an extravagant wife, a multitude of servants and a pack of hounds, as well as extensive alterations to the fine old house he had inherited. Completely changed since Roger Nowell's day, the present Read Hall, built about 1825, must be one of the finest houses in the north which is still in private hands and not accessible to the weekend public.

Three miles north-west of Whalley is Clitheroe and there, in the church of St Mary Magdalen, is a small but tangible memorial to John Webster. He spent his last years studying and writing near Clitheroe having at this time, in his own words, 'more converse with the dead than the living, more with books than with men', and on the wall of the church is a brass plate, bearing the symbols and inscription reproduced on page 162. Those who understand this figure, he says, will know me to have understood it too. Since those who have offered advice as

159

'Witches Galore' are still to be found at Newchurch

to its full significance have given explanations widely different and gone so far in one case as to interpret part of the inscription as an invocation against vampires we must leave the mystery with the reader.

The road from Whalley through Clitheroe leads over the border into Craven and the first Yorkshire village of Gisburn. Here is some trace of the Listers who harassed Jennet Preston. They were ancestors of later Lords Ribblesdale and in 1635 built the large house in the village street which is now the Ribblesdale Arms. A stone directly over the front door records this fact and the Lister family tree is in the main bar downstairs. It begins with John Lister of Derby in 1312 but omits the interesting fact that his wife, Isobel, claimed descent from Lady Godiva of Coventry fame.

From Gisburn the road back into Pendle passes Newfield Edge where Jennet Deane was bewitched out of her mind. There are at least three Newfield Edges in the area but from a gravestone in Ghyll Church at Barnoldswick it is possible to identify this as the home of the Deanes.

It was not, however, to Roughlee or Read or Malkin Tower that the crowds flocked in 1612, but to Lancaster, to the castle for the trial and the ceremonies of the Assizes, then to the gallows for the final drama. Lancaster Castle last had any real connection with royalty in the fifteenth century, during the reign of Henry IV. By the time of Henry VIII, like many castles left in the care of sheriffs, it had come to be used to house prisoners. Thomas Covell had charge of these for forty-eight years. Whether or not his wealth and eminence derived from his position as gaoler, or the fact that he was six times mayor of Lancaster, he has left his mark on the town. There is a memorial in the Priory Church of Lancaster which is next door to the castle. Two brasses now on a wall in the room at the bottom of the tower show his likeness and tell briefly of his attainments; their worn condition indicates that they were originally fastened to the church floor, over the place where he was buried. In

L   161

Those who understand this figure will
know me to have understood it too.

Here lies a man unknown and sunken
in a sea of contumely, yet bore it well
and cherished much of times gone by,
that he might learn the secrets of
wise men and come to know what
fire and water do.

John Hyphantes* or Webster, in
Spinosa, his country house among the
hills in a woodland Yorkshire parish
where the cuckoo sings.
Born Feb 3 1610, and parted from
this life at 72, June 18 1682.
And thus on his deathbed bade farewell
to this world.
Golden peace to the living and
eternal rest to the dead.

With fire and water he will at last
be restored to grace.

Qui hanc figurum intelligunt
Me etiam intellexisse, intelligent.

Hic jacet ignotus mundo, mersusque
  tumultu
Invidiæ, semper mens tamen æqua
  fuit.
Multa tulit veterum ut sciret secreta
  sophorum
Ac tandem vires noverit ignis aquæ.

Johannes Hyphantes sive Webster,
In villa Spinosa supermontane, in
Parochia silvæcuculatæ, in agro
Eboracensi, natus 1610 Feb. 3.
Ergastulum animæ deposuit 1682,
  Junii 18
Annog. ætatis suæ 72 currente.
Sicq. peroravit moriens mundo huic
  valedicans,
Aurea pax vivis, requies æterna
  sepultis.

Aqua cum Igna Tandem in gratium
  Redit.

* Webster's favourite signature, or pen-name.

Webster's Memorial, Clitheroe

The inscription over the front porch of the Ribblesdale Arms, Gisburn
(illustrated on page 79)

1911 the floor was reconstructed as part of the general church renovation, the plates moved, and all remains reinterred. Near the church and castle is Covell Cross which replaced an earlier cross on the same site and behind this is a fine old house, New Hall, at one time in Covell's possession and the place where for many years Assize judges lodged.

Parts of the castle are nowadays open to visitors and the very interesting conducted tour includes the inevitable trip to the dungeons, where those with sufficient motive can enjoy the

163

thrill of being temporarily locked in the dark along with others so inclined. However, these dungeons, originally Norman storehouses, are not the ones where the witches were held. They were put in the Well Tower, sometimes still called the 'Witches' Tower'. This, unfortunately, is in that part of the castle now, once again, being used as a prison. With the helpful co-operation of the prison governor and his deputy, and the reluctant permission of the Home Office (given only after we had enlisted the help of our Member of Parliament), we were able to see this cell where the Lancashire Witches awaited their trial, and where probably Demdike died. The Well Tower is north of the main gateway of the castle, and is easily distinguished from outside, being much older than the adjacent parts. It was probably built in the thirteenth century, during the reign of King John. Along with the keep, Hadrian's Tower, and the lower part of the gateway, it is all that remains of the medieval castle. It takes its name from a deep well just inside the entrance door from the courtyard. Into this well is channelled rain from the castle roof, with the practical purpose, in days when castles were liable to siege, of supplying drinking water for those inside.

Beneath the tower, and reached by a flight of stone steps, is a dungeon measuring twenty feet by twelve. The level floor consists of heavy blocks of dressed stone, and still fastened firmly to two of the middle ones are heavy iron rings, an inch thick and over six inches in diameter; spaces between the stones would allow water to run away. The roof of the dungeon is arched and was constructed by laying faggots in the shape required, then pouring mortar over the whole; it has been as free from wear as the roof of a deep cave and consequently the impressions of the sticks which made up the faggots are still sharply defined. The roof is about five feet high at the sides but over seven feet in the middle. We found the dungeon reasonably warm and dry and, having come to think with sympathy of the main characters of our book, were relieved to find that at least

Lancaster Castle: the steps to the dungeon

the additional trials of cold and damp were not added to the horrors of darkness, and the discomforts caused by lack of ventilation and sanitation.

From this dungeon on Thursday, 19 August 1612 those to be hanged were taken to the place of execution for the county. This was about a mile from the castle on a site now overbuilt by an extension to Lancaster Royal Grammar School, and the journey would involve a procession going through the doubtless crowded streets of the old town. From 1800, hangings (still public) were carried out at the castle itself, in a corner con-

In this dungeon below the Well Tower at Lancaster Castle the witches awaited trial and probably Demdike died

veniently situated so that the graveyard of the neighbouring church served as a grandstand for the spectators. They continued into the latter half of the nineteenth century, the last public hanging at Lancaster being in 1865. The monstrous and protracted exhibitions had attracted the crowds for many centuries and probably never more compellingly than on that August day in 1612 when the lives of the Pendle witches were brought to an unjust and undignified end.

Bibliography

Ainsworth, William Harrison. *The Lancashire Witches* (a novel), 1848.
Baines, Edward. *History of the County Palatine and Duchy of Lancaster*, 1836.
Bennett, Walter. *The History of Burnley*, Burnley, 1947.
The Pendle Witches, Burnley, 1957.
Blakey, Jesse. *Annals and Stories of Barrowford*, Nelson, 1929.
Boguet, Henri. *An Examen of Witches*, Lyons, 1602. English translation, London, 1929.
Brigg, Mary. 'The Forest of Pendle in the Seventeenth Century' (*Transactions of the Historic Society of Lancashire and Cheshire*, Vols 113, 115), Liverpool, 1962 and 1964.
Burland, Cottie A. *The Magical Arts*, 1966.
Gardner, Gerald Brosseau. *Witchcraft Today*, 1955.
The Meaning of Witchcraft, 1959.
Glass, Justine. *Witchcraft, the Sixth Sense and Us*, 1966.
Hole, Christina. *Witchcraft in England*, 1945.
A Mirror of Witchcraft, 1957.
Hopkins, Matthew. *The Discovery of Witches*, 1647.
Hughes, Pennethorne. *Witchcraft*, 1952.
James VI & I. *Demonology*, Edinburgh, 1597.
Leland, Charles Godfrey. *Aradia, or the Gospel of the Witches*, 1899.
Maple, Eric. *The Dark World of Witches*, 1962.
Miller, Arthur. *The Crucible* (a play), New York, 1953.

BIBLIOGRAPHY

Murray, Margaret A. *The Witch Cult in Western Europe*, Oxford, 1921.
The God of the Witches, 1933.
Neill, Robert. *Mist over Pendle* (a novel), 1951.
Witch Bane (a novel), 1967.
Notestein, Wallace. *History of Witchcraft in England, from 1558 to 1718*, Washington, 1911.
Parrinder, Geoffrey. *Witchcraft*, 1958.
Potts, Thomas. *The Wonderful Discovery of Witches in the County of Lancaster*, 1613.
Robbins, Rossell Hope. *The Encyclopedia of Witchcraft and Demonology*, 1959.
Scot, Reginald. *Discovery of Witchcraft*, 1584.
Scott, Sir Walter. *Letters on Demonology and Witchcraft*, 1830.
Sprenger, Jacob, and Kramer, Heinrich. *Malleus Maleficarum*, Cologne, 1486.
Summers, Montague. *Witchcraft and Black Magic*, 1946.
Walton, Jean. *Pendle Forest Folk*, Nelson, 1950.
Webster, John. *The Displaying of Supposed Witchcraft*, 1677.
Whitaker, T. D. *History of Whalley*, 1818.
Anonymous. *News from Scotland, Declaring the Damnable Life of Dr Fian, a Notable Sorcerer*, 1591.

Besides Thomas Potts' *Discovery of Witches*, republished in 1845 (Vol 6, Old Series), the following Chetham Society volumes:
The Journal of Nicholas Assheton, Vol 14, Old Series, 1848.
The Farington Papers, Vol 39, Old Series, 1856.
Stewards' House and Farm Accounts of the Shuttleworths of Smithills and Gawthorpe, Vols 35, 41, 43, 46, Old Series, 1856–8.
Materials for the History of Lancashire, Vol 61, New Series, 1907.

Diary of Events, 1612

BECAUSE of the precise way in which Thomas Potts copied the depositions given to the various Justices of the Peace it is possible to construct this diary.

Wed, 18 Mar. Alizon Device, on her way through Colne on a begging expedition, accused of laming by witchcraft John Law, a pedlar from Halifax.

Sat, 21 Mar. John Law's son, Abraham, received a letter from Colne telling of his father's condition.

Sun, 29 Mar. Abraham Law, having journeyed from Halifax, sought out Alizon Device and brought her to Colne to see his father.

Mon, 30 Mar. Alizon, her mother Elizabeth and brother James taken to Read by Abraham Law and examined by Roger Nowell. Alizon held, the others released.

Thurs, 2 April. Demdike, Chattox and Anne Redfearn questioned at Fence by Roger Nowell. All three detained.

At York, Jennet Preston of Gisburn acquitted and released after being charged with murder by witchcraft.

Sat, 4 April. Demdike, Chattox, Anne Redfearn and Alizon Device despatched to Lancaster.

Good Friday, 10 April. Meeting, at noon, of twenty or more friends and relatives of the prisoners, at Malkin Tower.

Wed, 15 April. Robert Holden heard evidence against the Samlesbury Witches.

Mon, 27 April. Roger Nowell, with Nicholas Bannister of Altham, set up an enquiry at the house of James Wilsey at Fence. Elizabeth Device, James Device and Jennet Device questioned, mostly about the Good Friday meeting at Malkin Tower.

(Details and dates of the arrest of others, such as Alice Nutter, and their despatch to Lancaster along with Elizabeth and James, are not recorded.)

Tues, 5 May. Three magistrates, Roger Nowell, Nicholas Bannister and Robert Holden reported as meeting together, place unspecified.

Tues, 19 May. Chattox and James Device again examined in Lancaster Castle by William Sandes, the mayor, Thomas Covell, the gaoler, and James Anderton, a Justice of the Peace.

Sun, 12 July. At Windle, evidence taken by Sir Thomas Gerard in the separate case of Isobel Roby.

Mon, 27 July. Jennet Preston tried at York for the murder of Thomas Lister. Found guilty.

Wed, 29 July. Jennet Preston hanged at York.

Fri, 7 Aug. More evidence against the Samlesbury Witches taken by Robert Holden.

Sun, 9 Aug. Jennet Booth of Padiham gave evidence to Nicholas Bannister against Margaret Pearson.

Sun, 16 Aug. In the afternoon Judges Bromley and Altham arrived at Lancaster from Kendal.

Mon, 17 Aug. Assizes opened.

Tues, 18 Aug. Trial of witches started in the afternoon. All these cases heard by Judge Bromley.

Tues, 18 Aug. Chattox, Elizabeth Device and James Device tried separately. All found guilty.

Anne Redfearn tried and acquitted.

Wed, 19 Aug. Trial of the Samlesbury Witches.

Anne Redfearn tried on a second charge.

Trials of Alice Nutter and Katherine Hewitt.

Salmesbury Witches found not guilty, the others guilty.

John and Jane Bulcock, Alizon Device, Margaret Pearson and Isobel Roby all tried in the afternoon.

Bulcocks acquitted, others found guilty.

All the convicted prisoners brought before the judge to receive their sentences.

Thurs, 20 Aug. Those sentenced to death taken from the castle and hanged.

Mon, 16. Nov Thomas Potts' account of the trials finished.

The Supposed Victims of Witchcraft

THIS was the bill of mortality of the witches' victims, as collected from the pages of Potts.

Robert Nutter of Greenhead, a victim of Old Chattox.
Richard Assheton of Downham, Old Demdike.
Richard Baldwin's child, Wheathead, also Demdike.
John Device ⎱
Anne Nutter ⎰
John Moore, infant, of Higham ⎰ all victims of Chattox.
Hugh Moore of Higham ⎰

John Robinson, nicknamed Swyer, of Barley ⎱ killed by the
James Robinson, his brother ⎰ witchcraft of
Elizabeth Device.
Henry Mitton of Roughlee, victim of Alice Nutter, in concert with
    Demdike and Elizabeth Device.
Anne Towneley, wife of Henry Towneley of Carr ⎱
John Duckworth ⎰ all four victims
John Hargreaves of Go ldshawBooth ⎰ of James Device.
Blaze Hargreaves of Higham ⎰
Christopher Nutter of Greenhead, killed by the witchcraft of Anne
    Redfearn.
Anne Foulds of Colne, death attributed to Katherine Hewitt.
Thomas Lister of Gisburn, killed by the witchcraft of Jennet Preston.

APPENDIX 3

Cuttings from Family Trees

THE DEMDIKES

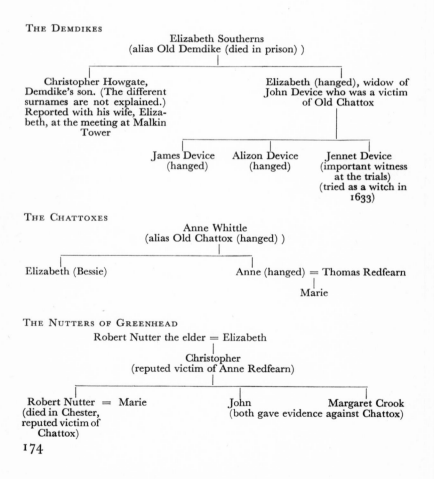

Elizabeth Southerns
(alias Old Demdike (died in prison))

Christopher Howgate,
Demdike's son. (The different
surnames are not explained.)
Reported with his wife, Eliza-
beth, at the meeting at Malkin
Tower

Elizabeth (hanged), widow of
John Device who was a victim
of Old Chattox

James Device
(hanged)

Alizon Device
(hanged)

Jennet Device
(important witness
at the trials)
(tried as a witch in
1633)

THE CHATTOXES

Anne Whittle
(alias Old Chattox (hanged))

Elizabeth (Bessie)

Anne (hanged) = Thomas Redfearn

Marie

THE NUTTERS OF GREENHEAD

Robert Nutter the elder = Elizabeth

Christopher
(reputed victim of Anne Redfearn)

Robert Nutter = Marie
(died in Chester,
reputed victim of
Chattox)

John
(both gave evidence against Chattox)

Margaret Crook

174

APPENDIX 3

THE LISTERS OF GISBURN

Thomas Lister
died 1607, supposed victim of Jennet Preston
|
Thomas Lister
died 1619, gave evidence against Jennet Preston, married to
Jane Heber of Marton, whose father Thomas Heber was
the magistrate responsible for Jennet's prosecution
|
Thomas Lister
died 1642, built, in 1635, the house which is now the Ribblesdale Arms

APPENDIX 4

Witchcraft in Britain Today

MOST victims of the trials, whether in Britain or elsewhere, were innocent of any connection with witchcraft. What the witch-hunters were looking for, and were often determined to find, was evidence of a crime which they had largely invented and embellished themselves. But there must have been practising witches living through the long years of the persecution, because true witchcraft is a very old religion which still survives and indeed shows new signs of flourishing in many countries—Britain included.

Authors who purport to give an account of an understandably secretive organisation to which they do not belong must admit that it will be incomplete. There are other handicaps. As witches form a religious group, seeking by however unorthodox a way that peace which passes all understanding, it goes without saying that they have their schisms. They disagree vehemently, not only about such things as the relative value of publicity as against close-kept silence, but about the very nature of the craft itself.

On the other hand many books and articles published in recent years have given the layman an insight into this intriguing faith. While some of the material is sensational and nasty, or so cautiously written that it presents an insipid picture of what is obviously a robust religion, most of it is sober and readable, and recently *Life* magazine devoted twelve pages to a review of witchcraft in Britain which earned the praises of the witches

176

themselves. From these various writings it is possible to build up a picture of the craft as it exists today.

Two important sources of information have been the books of the late Dr Brosseau Gardner (*The Meaning of Witchcraft* and *Witchcraft Today*) and the magazine *Pentagram*. Gardner set out to bring a greater measure of mutual understanding and unity of purpose to the surviving members of a fragmented cult, maintaining that as some covens are strong on theology, some on ritual, and others on occult technique, all would benefit from knowing more about the others. He had such an effect on the craft that some covens, those influenced by him or even started as the result of his work, are slightingly referred to by the more orthodox as 'Gardnerian'. He was something of a showman and contrived fairly frequent television appearances. However, he seems to have been liked, even by those who deplored the publicity he attracted to himself and to witches generally and who regarded some of his claims as the ramblings of an old man. He was a self-taught anthropologist, and would admit 'I am not a doctor really—just an honorary—for a book I wrote in Malaya.' He died at sea in 1964, on his way home from the Lebanon, and is buried in Tunis.

But our account has been greatly strengthened by a fortunate circumstance. Through a series of chance encounters, our search for witches who died over three hundred years ago led us to two practising witches who are much alive today. First approaches were greeted with pardonable suspicion: a previous interview, granted to an apparently earnest and sincere young man, had been followed by a sensational and inaccurate article in a Sunday newspaper.

Lois, an hereditary witch, is the High Priestess of a coven of which her husband is a member. (Their acknowledgment of themselves as witches confirms that the word is used for both men and women, contrary to the popular belief that a man should be called a wizard or warlock. These latter are magicians, and although witches may work to produce effects which would conventionally be termed 'magical', their methods are quite different.) We have never asked to be admitted to any secrets and none have been volunteered, but this appendix has been written in the knowledge that it could be submitted for correction and approval to two friendly and candid members of the cult it briefly describes.

Although in outward appearance witches are unremarkable (unless like Gerald Gardner they trim their beard and train their hair to look more devilish for each television appearance), it would be a mistake to describe them as ordinary. They have never acknowledged the limitations of the material world. They are keenly aware of the subtle forces which are apparent to those with psychic powers, and they aim in their ceremonies at a religious ecstasy which can be interpreted as a brief union of their soul with their gods. This aim is common to most branches of occultism, and the rapturous experience is claimed to enrich and flavour workaday life for a long time afterwards.

Theirs is a religion which rejects the teachings of original sin, vicarious atonement, and salvation by faith. They accept personal responsibility for their actions which cannot be expunged by confessions or penances. They believe in reincarnation and are therefore not afraid to die, but hope that this life has merited their being born again, after a period of rest and refreshment, amongst their own kind—a belief, then, similar to the Hindu doctrine of Karma. Witchcraft is pagan and pantheistic. It is also a mystery religion and a fertility cult. As Christian spines have been conditioned to shudder at these words we should consider exactly what they imply.

A pagan is one who does not worship the God of the Christian, the Muslim or the Jew, and since witchcraft claims to be as old a religion as any in the world, pre-dating even Judaism, it must be pagan. To say that it is pantheistic is to impute no more than a belief that God permeates all things. It fits the description of a mystery religion, of which there were many in the ancient world, because its experiences are only for the initiate.

Primitive societies cannot turn to scientists to better their crops, or to doctors to improve the health of their offspring; yet they desire as much as we do to have full bellies, and lusty youngsters to carry on the race. For them these matters are dealt with by the priests, and the rituals prescribed to ensure that the wheat yields abundantly, and that the race survives, or even the sun returns in the summer, are what we call fertility rites. Modern witches, as scientifically minded as the rest of us, claim that without changing their basic beliefs, many of their old rites have been easily adapted to the present time, and that their simple and beautiful religion, now concerned with spiritual rather than material fertility, provides a refreshing escape from the stress of modern life, which is in danger of cutting us off from nature, or as they poetically put it, 'orphaning us from the great mother'.

The craft has no central organisation. Although there are lone practitioners, witches generally belong to an autonomous group, or coven. This need not number thirteen although this number is considered ideal and once it is reached the group will most likely split into two smaller ones. A coven is a group of like-minded people, many from families that have practised witchcraft for centuries, others drawn to its pattern of ritual and worship. Members meet regularly and in secret, and most of them ask only to be left alone, rejecting alike the intrusion of the ignorant and unsympathetic, the authority (which they deny) of a recently proclaimed 'Queen of the Witches', and even the earnest attempts of those who simply desire to see them better acquainted with each other.

As witchcraft is a matriarchal religion we find a woman, usually elected by the others, as High Priestess—head and supreme authority in each coven. She chooses a man as High Priest, an office of particular importance at some of their main festivals. Her deputy is called the 'maiden'.

Witches worship a god and a goddess, admitting that these are symbols or images used to enable the limited human mind to form some conception of divinity. They take an oath never to reveal the names they use for them—a custom and a protection against outsiders' taking the names in vain. But they will speak of them as the Horned God and the Moon, or Mother Goddess. These forms are probably amongst the oldest representations of divinity in the world and have been worshipped, under different names and guises, at least since the Stone Age. They are not regarded as all-powerful, but looked upon as vehicles of power which can only operate in conjunction with men or women initiated into their mysteries.

The attraction of the idea of a goddess—the comforting, embracing mother—is surely acknowledged by the prominence given to Mary by the Roman Catholic Church. Yet, while a place can be found for a woman, the Christian God could brook no male rivals, and instead of being assimilated the god of the old religion became the Devil of the new, and the horned deity of the witches was identified with God's adversary, Satan, a possible origin of the idea that the Devil has horns.

Witches stress that they do not believe in the existence of either the Devil or Hell. The question of paying homage to the former, or worshipping him, does not therefore arise. As Gardner says: 'Witches do not kiss the Devil's posterior, first because they never kiss anyone's posterior and secondly because the Devil is never there for anyone to kiss!' Neither are they interested in performing blasphemous parodies of Christian ceremonies. Again to quote Gardner: 'The witches' rites in no way resemble those of any church I know; there are no inverted crucifixes or mock sermons, no praise or homage to the Devil, no evil liturgy, nothing is said backwards, and there are no gestures with the left hand.' No matter what Black Masses have been said, graves opened, cocks sacrificed, or effigies nailed to church doors, these are not the works of genuine witches, although as in days of old, when such goings-on come to

180

light, the public and the press carelessly call them witchcraft.

The unsupported, and strongly denied, suggestions that witchcraft entitles its members to take part in regular promiscuous revelry naturally attracts many whose interests are far removed from the world of the spirit. These would-be converts should join one or other of the bogus covens which have sprung up from time to time and which have even advertised for members. A genuine witch coven does not actively seek new members. 'We do not exist to convert people to a belief in the Goddess, but rather to give those who already know her an opportunity to meet together and adore her.' They believe that anyone who is unknowingly a witch will be drawn naturally to their circle, and that to initiate a person who is spiritually out of tune would not only be no benefit to her, but would serve to hinder their work. Once initiated it is hardly surprising that the secrecy of the organisation, the long road perhaps travelled to find it, and the admitted ecstasy generated at the meetings, should develop amongst members a close and loving bond much stronger than is to be found in most societies, until, in fact, they come to regard themselves as belonging to a class apart.

Initiations usually take place at one of the four great festivals: Candlemas (the beginning of February), May Eve (also called Beltane or Walpurgis Night), Lammas (1 August) and, as is common knowledge, Hallowe'en (31 October). These festivals divide the year into four more or less exact quarters, and each celebration marks, far more realistically than our equinoxes and solstices, the beginning of a season. At an initiation a man is introduced by a woman and vice-versa, the only exceptions being that a mother can bring in her daughter, or a father his son. Initiation does not in itself convey any actual power. Continual participation in the rites, in association with others, is considered to tend to release and develop any psychic faculties in those in whom they are latent.

Before an initiation a charge is read. This begins: 'Listen to the words of the Great Mother, who was of old called amongst men Artemis, Astarte, Aphrodite, Diana and many other names. At mine altars the youths of Lacedemon and Sparta made due sacrifice. Whenever you have need of anything, once in a month, and better it be when the moon is full, then shall ye assemble in some secret place. . . .' The charge ends: '. . . if that which thou seekest thou findest not within thee, thou wilt never find it without thee, for behold I have been with thee from the beginning, and I am that which is attained at the end of all desire.'

The craft tradition, mostly for secrecy's sake, has for long been almost entirely oral. There are no scriptures except for the *Book of Shadows*. This is copied by each witch in her own hand, unless passed down from parent to child, and is destroyed when the owner dies. It gives details of secret rites, contains much herbal knowledge, and something of the history of the craft. It also includes spells—but more about these when we come to the working of magic.

Each month, as near to full moon as can be, but never when the moon is on the wane, witches assemble for their regular sabbat. On rare occasions if the weather is suited, and if secrecy can be maintained, they meet outdoors. But as neither of these conditions can often be relied upon in civilised Britain, the meeting is usually indoors, in a room swept clean and made warm in readiness. A circle, roughly nine feet in diameter, but varying with the size of the group, is marked on the ground in chalk, tape or rope. Inside the circle will be a simple altar on which stand salt, water, a platter of biscuits and sometimes a statuette of the Goddess. There will be incense-burners, candles, a wine cup, a wand, knife and sword, a pentacle (a device much favoured by magicians as well as witches), and a scourge, the last for symbolic purification. Each coven has a set of tools for ritual use, treasured as are the altar ornaments in a church. In addition each witch has a black-handled knife called an Athame which she is encouraged to make herself, unless she has inherited one.

182

The circle is outlined with the point of a knife or sword, then purified with water and incense. The candles on the altar, and four which are outside the circle, are lit. A prayer is said to the Goddess to grant their wishes, then the others join the High Priestess inside the circle, she greeting and purifying them as they enter. Most covens do as they are charged and work naked, except for the necklaces of the women.

The ritual is long, exciting and tiring. The rhythms of the dance, the mutual sympathy and common motive of the dancers, the incense, and the strong scent used by the women and now given off as bodies are heated by dancing, build up to an intense, intoxicating climax, when, as one of them said, 'It is as if the Goddess had brushed against my soul, I am filled with deep happiness and joy and good will, that subsequent cares and tribulations can never quite erase. I feel the continuity of my life with the past and present and its harmony and rhythm with the earth and seasons.'

Many of their practices and claims are far outside what most people accept as normal. But the exhilarating properties of a pulsating rhythm, accompanied by dancing, or variants such as the Dervishes' whirling or the Sufis' intense rhythmic breathing, have long been known to primitive people. They will be better understood by today's young people in their strident, throbbing cellars, than by those to whom dancing means the graceful but inhibited steps of the ballroom.

Part of the purpose of the sabbat is to work magic, usually to help or heal some member of the coven. Rites vary according to their purpose, but to achieve results the gods need power. Here we have the explanation of the nakedness, the consecrated circle, and the necessity, in this type of rite, of working in pairs. Power is generated by the woman; the man, acting as an earth to an electrical impulse, brings it down and makes it usable. As for the nakedness, witches regard the human body as a storehouse of energy and believe that clothes would hinder its release. The circle keeps in bounds the 'cone of power' which is built up, then directed to achieve their ends. In this respect it is quite different from the circle of the sorcerer. His was to protect himself from the powerful and often terrible spirits he was invoking to do his work.

This directing of power is what can be called 'casting a spell'; and to the charge that this power could equally be channelled to bad ends, the witches answer that, although magic is a neutral force which can be used for good or ill, it would be against their law of love to all beings to work evil magic. Obedience to this law engenders a quality clumsily, but accurately, described as 'hurtlessness'. It is an attitude similar to that preached by Gandhi and his followers and called by them 'ahimsa'.

We cannot describe in more detail rituals we have never witnessed. We are intrigued, like other laymen, by Gardner's statement that a sabbat is no place to take your maiden aunt 'even if she is a romantic'. 'Fine but primitive things happen,' he says, 'which would distress a Puritan.' 'Ours,' he says, 'is a religion of love, pleasure and excitement, we worship the divine spirit of creation whose command was: "Go forth and multiply".'

Anyone who is sufficiently interested to read even a few of the many hundreds of books devoted wholly or in part to witchcraft will form his own opinions about the wilder assertions and theories he will find. One book claims, for instance, that by a massing of witches' wills in 1940, the idea was put into Hitler's head that he should not invade Britain. The same technique we are told had been successfully used against Napoleon and before that, in 1588, against the Armada: although they disclaim responsibility for the stormy seas which were partly responsible for the Spanish fleet's undoing, the theory goes, the witches tried hard, and evidently successfully, to prevent the Spaniards from landing. Our friends within the cult describe these claims as rubbish. Another interesting, but dubious, theory from the witch books is that Britannia on a banknote, holding an ear of corn, is derived from the Mother Goddess of fertility.

184

APPENDIX 4

The authors compass the whole range of intelligence and integrity, from Dr Margaret Murray, who asserts that all England's kings, at least as far as the Plantagenets, were initiates of the old religon, down to those writers who interpret the placing of a wedding ring on the bride's finger as symbolic of the sex act, and see phallic symbolism in everything from maypoles to ballpoint pens.

Just one more is worth mentioning. Gerald Gardner puts forward an explanation for the popular association of witches with broomsticks. A witch would be hired to enact a ceremony to make the crops grow. One form of this was to put a pole or broom between her legs to represent a phallus, and thus equipped to leap around over the growing corn, symbolically fertilising it and drawing it out of the ground. Before feeling too superior about these antics of our ancestors we should remember that they belong originally to an age without artificial fertilisers or even efficient ploughs. And anyone who throws confetti at a wedding is performing the pale shadow of a fertility rite. Confetti has largely replaced rice, which was thrown in the hope that the newly-consecrated union of a man and woman would be as fruitful as the rice itself.

Even now that, in our tolerant age, witches can proclaim their faith before millions on television, the word 'witch' is still evocative, and though a confessed witch will no longer find herself led to the gallows, or tied to a stake with a pile of faggots for company, the closed minds of the orthodox can find insidious and subtle forms of persecution. This is the reason why many witches deplore the recent publicity. Many worthy citizens would have misgivings about a woman who declared herself to be a witch, shut herself away at regular intervals with other men and women of her faith, and refused to say exactly what she did. The combination of secrecy and nakedness is too much for them. Yet highly respectable freemasons, whose aims are far removed from the making of magic or the attaining of ecstasy, enjoy their own particular ritual and secrecy. They meet behind closed and guarded doors, they have secret signs of recognition, and books and regalia for the initiated only. Both societies have degrees within themselves, and a scene from a recent television programme supposed to portray the installation of a mason, was very closely matched in a newspaper picture about the same time on the initiation of a witch; blindfold, bared breast, sword and all!

Witches have a saying, 'An' it harm none, do what thou wilt', and so long as what they do brings joy to them and injury to none, they have surely the right to be left alone.

Acknowledgments

FOR their help in the preparation of this book we particularly wish to thank: Wilfred Spencer, chairman, Colne Local History Society, who introduced us to each other and whose knowledge of local history and its sources has saved us many hours of searching; Mary Brigg for her help with the background history of Pendle Forest; and Lois Pearson for so generously giving us an insight into modern witchcraft.

In addition, for their help in various ways, we offer our grateful thanks to: The Governor of HM Prison at Lancaster; the late Sydney Silverman, former Member of Parliament for Nelson and Colne; the librarian and staff of Colne Public Library; Tom Pemberton and colleagues, Art Teacher Training Dept, Leeds College of Art; the owners of Malkin Tower, Greenhead, Saddler's and Dam Head Farms for allowing us access to their deeds. Also: Dr Frank Ayrey, Brian Bamber, Walter Bennett, Cottie Burland, Stuart Kay, Geoffrey Little and the office staff of R. G. Little & Co, Stuart Mason, David L. M. Parkinson, Ana and Richard Peel, James Southern, Cledwyn Thomas, Ann Whale and Colin Wharton, Frank Bannister and Dr Ken Cooper.

Index

Page references for illustrations are printed in italic

INDEX

INDEX

INDEX

Moore, John, 22, 32, 126
Moore, John (infant), 22, 32, 58, 173
Moss End Farm, 42, 46, 68, 155, *68*
Murray, Dr Margaret, 148, 185

Napier, Barbara, 33
Neill, Robert, 15, 64, 146
Newcastle on Tyne, 36
Newchurch in Pendle, 13, 41–4, 68, 126, 146, 155, 157–8, 160, *12*, *158*, *160*
Newes from Scotland, 144
Newfield Edge, 68–9, 161
Norfolk Assizes, 101
Nowell, Alexander, 159
Nowell, Roger, 20–2, 26–34, 36, 38–43, 45–6, 49, 58, 60–1, 70–1, 78–9, 83, 87, 90–1, 143, 146–7, 159, 170–1
Nutter, Alice, 42, 46, 60, 85, 88–9, 128, 146–7, 151, 157, 171–3;trial, 49, 63–7, 74
Nutter, Anne, 22, 32, 58, 173
Nutter, Anthony, 22, 32
Nutter, Christopher, 16–17, 27, 30–1, 63, 152, 173–4
Nutter, Elizabeth, 30
Nutter, John (Greenhead), 16–17, 31, 63, 174
Nutter, John (Bull Hole), 21, 23, 126, 128, 142
Nutter, John (priest), 85
Nutter, Marie, 30, 174
Nutter, Myles, 42, 146
Nutter, Richard, 42, 64
Nutter, Robert (Greenhead), 16–17, 27, 30–1, 47, 58, 62, 152, 173–4
Nutter, Old Robert (Greenhead), 17, 27, 152, 174
Nutter, Robert (priest), 85

Old Laund, 157
'Old Religion', 124, 176–86
Ordeal, trial by, 36, 50–1

Padiham, 19, 42, 49, 71–2, 74, 95–6, 141–2, 146, 171
Pearson, Edward, 146
Pearson, Margaret, 90, 141–2, 146, 172; trial of, 49, 71–4, 172
Pendle Forest, 11, 13, 16, 18–19, 26–8, 41, 94–5, 97, 125, 147–51, 154–6, 161, *24–5* (map)
Pendle Hill, 9, 10, 61, 149–50
Pendle Water, 9, 152
Pendle Witches, *see* Lancashire Witches
Pentagram, 178

Pillory, 52, 72–4, *73*
Poor Law Acts, 147
Possession by devils, 132–3, 135
Potts, Thomas, 74, 147, 170; *Discovery of Witches*, 11–13, 15, 89–93, 124–5, 142, 172–3; opinions or descriptions of: John and Jane Bullock, 89–90; Chattox, 58; Demdike, 23, 26–7; *Demonology*, 88; Alizon Device, 90; Elizabeth Device, 23, 45, 59, 89; Jennet Device, 60; James Device, 61, 89; Thomas Heber, 78; judges, 92; John Law, 69–70; Roger Nowell, 20, 41; Alice Nutter, 64–6; Margaret Pearson, 90; Pendle Forest, 150; Anne Redfearn, 89; Roman Catholics, 84; Christopher Southworth, 86–7; Grace Sowerbutts, 83, 86–7
Preston, Jennet, 41–2, 45, 147, 161, 170, 173, 175; trial at York, 77–82, 87, 171
Preston, 'Old', 81–2
'Pricking' of witches, 35–6, 100, 136, *37*
Public Record Office, 141

Ramsden, John, 50, 75, 82
Read, 20, 91–2, 133, 136, 146, 159, 170
Recusancy Laws, 85
Red Bank, 84
Redfearn, Anne, 16–18, 26, 30–2, 46, 49, 59, 89, 146, 152, 170, 173–4; trial of, 62–3, 67, 74, 171–2
Redfearn, Marie, 63
Redfearn, Thomas, 16–17, 30–1, 63, 152, 174
Remy, Nicholas, 121
Ribblesdale Arms, Gisburn, 161, 175, *79*, *163*
Robinson, Anne, 79–80
Robinson, Edmund (son), 94–9, 133
Robinson, Edmund (father), 96–8
Robinson, James (Barley), 46, 60, 173
Robinson, James (Greenhead), 31, 58
Robinson, John, 45–6, 60, 173
Roby, Isobel, 49, 148, 172; trial of, 74, 77, 88–9, 172
Roman Catholicism in Lancashire, 84–5
Rombalds (Romles) Moor, 81
Roughlee, 21, 42, 46, 60, 65, 146, 150, 152, 157, 173
Roughlee Hall, 64, 151–2, *64*

St Helens, 49, 88
St Osyth, 129

191

INDEX